THERAPEUTIC
YOGA
WORKS

A GENTLE APPROACH TO ELIMINATING BACK PAIN AND IMPROVING FUNCTIONAL MOBILITY FOR LIFE

By Nydia Tijerina Darby, DPT

Photographs by: Lisa Preston—@imageforager.com
Art Direction: Irene Maag Hernandez
ISBN: 979-8-89109-255-6 (paperback)
ISBN: 979-8-89109-398-0 (hardcover)
ISBN: 979-8-89109-256-3 (ebook)

PRAISE FOR *THERAPEUTIC YOGA WORKS*

"Dr. Darby and I have been colleagues for several decades and have taught many yoga workshops and teacher training programs together. After I had a hip replacement in 2010, she flew from Texas to New York to share her expertise in yoga therapeutics with me to aid in my speedy and stress-free recovery. Nydia's methodology of integrating yoga therapy and physical therapy is a unique and brilliant contribution to the world of pain management. This book is a gift to all those struggling with back pain. Read her stories and do the practices. It will change your life."

—Beryl Bender, Best-Selling Author of *Power Yoga*, Founder/Director of The Hard & The Soft Yoga Institute, and Co-Founder Give Back Yoga Foundation

"This book beautifully outlines what it would be like to work with Nydia using the Therapeutic Astanga Method© that she developed for helping to empower those who are healing low back pain. It demonstrates clearly the whole-person approach that she uses as a yoga therapist, and I think after reading it, you will feel quite comfortable scheduling a time to work with Nydia or those who have been trained by her."

—Amy Wheeler, Founder of Optimal State, Former President of the Board of the International Association of Yoga Therapists

"Nydia Darby has a passion for making the experience of yoga accessible to every BODY. This book puts forth Nydia's life work in a manner that expands her method outside the confines of her studio and into the reader's home. Working with Nydia has changed my life—both personally and professionally. Learning how to move and breathe 17 years ago with Nydia and her therapeutic yoga showed me another path to deal with the stresses of being a busy physician and mother to three small children. It also resolved my stress-induced migraines and has helped me through other challenges. Now with children grown and an eye towards my next decade, I am truly grateful for the wisdom of Nydia's therapeutic yoga lifestyle that helps me to enjoy every day."

—Simone Norris, MD, Founder of Integrative Family Medicine in San Antonio, Texas, USAF Veteran, and Graduate of Dr. Andrew Weil's Fellowship in Integrative Medicine

"This terrific book reveals how therapeutic yoga improves quality of life through self-care. Nydia Darby forever changed my life, which now includes my new role as primary caregiver. Her guidance helps me prevent injury while preserving and enhancing my mobility as I 'train for my next decade.'"

—Dr. Susan Blackwood, (Retired) Executive Director,
San Antonio Sports

"Nydia's integrated approach to wellness is grounded in her unique background as a physical therapist as well as a therapeutic yoga specialist. When a combination of severe spinal and muscular issues eliminated my ability to walk unassisted, Nydia's advice, private sessions, and group classes gave me both help and hope. Her guidance regarding the healing and balancing power of the mind/body/spirit connection helped restore my strength, mobility, and redirected my outlook on life. You are choosing joy when you choose to work with Nydia."

—Patti Larsen, Owner, Patti Larsen Consulting;
(Retired) Director, AT&T External & Legislative Affairs

"Important insights for those striving to practice optimal self-care."

—Ajeya Joshi, MD, Orthopedic Spine Surgeon and
Lifestyle Medicine Physician

"If you have a spine, this book is for you! Seriously! While written for the 8 out of 10 of us who have experienced, are experiencing, or will experience back pain, spasms, instability, and/or spinal dysfunction at some time in our lives, *Therapeutic Yoga Works* is the must-have body manual for anyone and everyone wanting to improve and maintain body/mind/spirit balance, flexibility, strength, and vital well-being for life."

—Rita Millett Mikel, Certified Advanced Rolfer and
Owner of Source Coaching and Consulting

"Nydia says it all in the title of her book: *Therapeutic Yoga Works: A Gentle Approach to Eliminating Back Pain and Improving Functional Mobility for Life*. She offers a mindful, whole-person approach focused on reducing musculoskeletal imbalance and improving mobility for those living with spinal pain. Her unique, breath-centered technique helps create a form of movement meditation that also quiets our constant brain chatter and encourages healing from the inside-out."

—Ellen Lin, MD, Board-Certified Physical Medicine
and Rehabilitation Physician and Pain Management
Specialist

DOWNLOAD THE AUDIOBOOK FREE!

READ THIS FIRST

I want to thank you for purchasing my book and would like to give you the audiobook version 100% FREE!
I really want you to finish this book and have narrated the audiobook myself to give you another tool to help you move towards balance and well-being.

THERAPEUTICYOGAWORKS.COM/AUDIO

FREE VIDEO ACCESS TO THE THERAPEUTIC YOGA PRACTICES IN THIS BOOK!

I want you to have a positive experience with your therapeutic yoga practice, so I have created a platform where you can view and follow along while I guide you through the activities that I am sharing in this book.

You can also download a PDF of the practices that you will see in Chapter 11 to help support your success with your Therapeutic Yoga practice.

Go to TherapeuticYogaWorks.com to get instant access to the videos and to join my monthly newsletter.

THERAPEUTICYOGAWORKS.COM

To David, Jake, and Michelina—your love, support, and encouragement lift me up every day.

You are what your deep driving desire is. As is your desire, so is your will. As is your will, so is your deed. As is your deed, so is your destiny.

—Upanishads: Brihadaranyaka IV.5

TABLE OF CONTENTS

FOREWORD

NYDIA DARBY—MY FRIEND, TEACHER, AND RESEARCH PARTNER

By Amelie G. Ramirez

It is my pleasure to know Nydia as a friend, teacher, and research partner for over 25 years.

I first met her when she was an exercise instructor at a fitness center. Her sessions were always the most popular. She was always cautious about posture and how you approached each exercise to make sure you attained the full benefits without hurting yourself.

When Nydia opened her own yoga studio, I signed up right away.

As a health promotion researcher, I've always tried to be a role model for two important keys to a healthy lifestyle—eating right and doing physical activity.

But I don't like to run long distances. Power lifting is not for me. I dread two hours on the elliptical.

Yoga became my path to staying healthy.

Nydia helped me along that path. Her teaching style is kind and welcoming. Her therapeutic approach to yoga empowers me and others toward improving functionality, easing pain, and developing a more energetic body. Her mantra of synthesizing the whole person—mind, body, spirit—is one that resonates with me as I seek wellness over the long term.

Everyone deserves this kind of experience.

In fact, in Nydia's studio one day, I had an idea how to apply it more broadly.

In my medical research experience, I'd long known that cancer survivors often struggle with staying healthy after their diagnosis and treatment. I knew that they are often scared or worried about how physical activity might affect them, even though physical activity is even more important after cancer. I thought, "Would therapeutic yoga like Nydia's be better than more traditional or general exercise at helping cancer survivors with their fitness and quality of life, and also help reduce their risk of future cancer or recurrence?"

I came to Nydia with an idea to build a research study to test different kinds of physical activity. She saw the value in assessing her approach and its benefits. In a yearlong study with 90 breast cancer survivors, Nydia and my team, with support from Susan G. Komen, evaluated her yoga intervention and other exercise programs. The results were fantastic. Nydia's therapeutic yoga was equally as effective as more traditional exercise methods for improving wellness among cancer survivors. For those interested, you can read about the study in the 2015 article entitled "Effect of a Six-Month Yoga Exercise Intervention on Fitness Outcomes for Breast Cancer Survivors" in the journal *Physiotherapy Theory and Practice*.

Nydia has continued to work with me, Dr. Daniel Hughes, and my team to create innovative ways to use therapeutic yoga to help people achieve better health, from livestreaming yoga sessions amid COVID-19 to our newest grant to test an integrative holistic approach (including yoga with meditation) to maximize outcomes for physical, mental, and spiritual aspects of the quality of life for Latina breast cancer survivors.

Nydia's book is a testament to the hard work she puts in and the passion she displays for teaching and helping people. She has a wonderful ability to share her innovative approach to yoga in an easy-to-read, easy-to-follow way.

I hope this book will enable everyone to incorporate therapeutic yoga into their daily lives. I know I will continue to do so. And I also know that I am looking forward to many more years of learning from Nydia, working with Nydia, and continuing our amazing friendship.

Namaste, friends.

Amelie

Amelie G. Ramirez, DrPH, of UT Health San Antonio, is a health equity pioneer who has achieved local, state, national, presidential, and international recognition for her successes in reducing Latino cancer health disparities and championing system and policy changes that promote health equity for Latinos. As leader of the Institute for Health Promotion Research and Chair and Full Professor of the

Department of Population Health Sciences at UT Health San Antonio, a Hispanic-Serving Institute, Ramirez leads a multidisciplinary team of public health researchers, data scientists, and communication specialists in addressing the cancer experience of Latinos. Dr. Ramirez leads the Salud America! communication program, www.salud-america.org, a national network of over 500,000 community, school, and healthcare leaders. Dr. Ramirez has been recognized by Oprah Winfrey, the Obama White House, the National Academy of Medicine, and more. Dr. Ramirez is a native of Laredo, Texas.

INTRODUCTION—TRAINING FOR YOUR NEXT DECADE

My name is Nydia Tijerina Darby, and I am an integrative physical therapist and therapeutic yoga specialist. I refer to myself as an "integrative physical therapist and therapeutic yoga specialist" because I integrate a variety of complementary approaches in the programs that I create for my patients and clients to empower them towards improved function, overall health, and long-term wellness. I teach them as much as they care to know about their physical and energetic bodies and support them in their personal process towards whole health for the long term. I refer to this as being in "training for the next decade."

I am writing this book to introduce a gentle approach to therapeutic yoga that is directed to those who may be suffering from low back pain, spasm, and/or instability, all of which fall into the area of spinal dysfunction. People who are ready to take action to learn how to help reduce their own suffering, who have tried other methods and failed to have long-term success and who are eager to improve their long-term well-being by incorporating gentle therapeutic yoga lifestyle practices into their self-care regimen. I am writing this book to share the gentle approach that I have developed over the last 40 years that considers the whole person, mind, body, and spirit, and to share this unique approach to wellness that is influenced by the physical therapy, fitness, and yoga practices that I have learned, led, taught, shared, and embodied over the last 40 years—the Therapeutic Astanga Method© that I regularly refer to as therapeutic yoga.

NYDIA'S BACKGROUND

I am a doctor of physical therapy who chose to work outside of the traditional medical system. I have been expanding my offerings to the local and global community with the mind, body, and spirit practices that I developed over the course of 40 years where I integrate a specialized therapeutic yoga practice into the programs that I offer. These programs are aimed at supporting and educating individuals and small groups who are ready to commit to improving their long-term functional mobility and health. I started with individual sessions, then began providing small group sessions to individuals with similar orthopedic concerns. Seventeen years ago, I expanded my offerings by opening and operating a yoga studio that was accessible to the local community. After 10 years, I moved my operations to a smaller, more convenient studio location to continue the process and focus attention on research and writing.

I was inspired to write this book when I realized that I was limited in the number of people that I could reach in my daily work offering live and livestreamed group therapeutic yoga sessions. Even though my work in therapeutic yoga and cancer research was improving my outreach and ability to share the method that I had developed, I also realized that few laypersons read scientific journals. It became very clear that I needed to write a book that could potentially put my work in the hands of those individuals who may not ever take a yoga class, but who might consider learning from my book. I focused this writing on back and spine care, even though this subject only touches a small segment of the conditions that I help my clients with.

THE JOURNEY OF THE BOOK

I'd like to give you a little insight into what you might expect to find as you read this book. In the chapters ahead, I share something that my yoga teacher once told me about starting a yoga practice—that you will never be the same again—in a good way. You can't say that I didn't warn you. ☺

I begin in Chapter 1 by sharing about myself and the process that inspired me to meld my experiences in physical therapy and fitness in my early professional days. My quest to find a process that would help me move gracefully through the next decades eventually brought me to yoga and, from there, I developed a unique approach to breath-centered movement awareness practices that I began to refer to as therapeutic yoga, the subject of this book.

In Chapters 2 through 9, you get to meet Caroline whose story reflects the experiences that I had with many clients that I have worked with over the past 40 years. Caroline is a beautiful soul who reaches out to me after being referred by one of my former clients. Caroline has been experiencing debilitating back pain and spasm over the course of many years. She is tired of hurting and is afraid of what lies in her future if she doesn't make a change. She doesn't know if it's possible to change, but she is willing to try anything, even yoga with a physical therapist. Therapeutic yoga is her last hope in the quest to get her life back. In these chapters, you will get a peek into what a private therapeutic yoga assessment and private therapeutic yoga sessions can be like for an individual suffering from back pain due to spinal instability and deconditioning. I share the practices that I used over the last 40 years that I know can have a beneficial effect on reducing spine pain and improving spine mobility and a person's functional abilities.

In sharing Caroline's story, I also address some of the concerns, fears, and hopes that she shares with me during our work together. Additionally, I have chosen to weave some of the practices into the story. That is on purpose. I want you to enter this world with us. I have also woven some observations and information that I hope will help you understand spine pain and dysfunction better. I want to help take the mystery out of spine pain and possibly improve your understanding of this unfortunately common condition. I am sharing this with you, the reader, like I would be sharing it with a client that is in my care. I believe that knowledge is POWER and that the more that we know about how our amazing body functions, in sickness and in health, the better.

In Chapter 10, I share tips and some notes that expand upon the ideas behind the methods that I have developed to help individuals with chronic conditions such as spine pain, spasm, and instability. These practices are considered adaptogenic because they are not limited to benefitting only those persons who are living with spine pain; they can also benefit and help to restore balance in the bodies of persons who suffer from many other conditions. I incorporate these movements into my own personal therapeutic yoga practice that I do every morning.

I have spent the last 40 years developing these specific variations of traditional exercise and yoga practices, and I know that the method that I am sharing works. I am confident that the postures and movements that I am providing in this book can help those who are willing to do the work to help themselves improve their mobility, stability, and possibly their long-term quality of life. Remember, check in with your health care team to let them know that you are considering starting this practice of gentle therapeutic yoga. Show them this book.

In the last chapter, you will find a list of every activity that I refer to in this book. You will see images of the postures with instructions. I provide this resource so that you might consider starting your own practice. I want you to be able to read the instructions and see the images of me doing the postures. Because it could be valuable for you to have a hard copy of the images and written descriptions of the yoga poses for easy reference when doing the practice, you can go to TherapeuticYogaWorks.com to access a PDF of this chapter. On this website you will also find videos that I created of each posture and select practices that I designed to help you get started on your therapeutic yoga program. I want you to do this practice. I want you to get strong, to be more mobile, and to be able to move freely with minimal discomfort for your entire life. I want you to do therapeutic yoga.

WHY STORYTELLING?

One last thing, before you move into the first chapter—to explain how the therapeutic yoga method works to alleviate pain and bring function and quality of life back to people, I purposefully chose to do this in a storytelling format through Caroline's sessions with me. Why storytelling and not something more technical and objective? Because I wanted to share something that the reader would find interesting and be informative at the same time. I decided to share the experience of what a private therapeutic yoga assessment and private integrative physical therapy session with me could be like. These sessions reflect the practice in that they involve the whole person, mind, body, and spirit. It just made sense to me to share Caroline's story.

I know that I need to write a technical book about the method that I have developed, the Therapeutic Astanga Method© that I am sharing in this book. I have a group of medical and yoga professionals whom I have trained and certified as TAM© informed yoga teachers. These trainings were delivered over the years via the Open Hand Institute, which is an extension of Nydia's Yoga Therapy Studio and the platform that I use to support the education and training of TAM© yoga professionals for therapeutic yoga research and the offering of therapeutic yoga programs for the community at large. These trained teachers have been waiting for the TAM© manual. I am grateful for their support and patience. In full disclosure, I started writing the TAM© technical manual before I realized that I wanted to introduce therapeutic yoga to the persons who were suffering from back pain, which is one of the most common challenges in our communities. I wanted to reach out to these persons in my first book and share this gentle therapeutic yoga method in a story. I felt that my first book should be directed to the reader who might want to see what therapeutic yoga is about without all the technical jargon. Some of you reading this will be happy to know that the TAM©

manual is waiting for me in my computer and is next in line for my future writing adventures.

Deciding what writing approach to use for this book just came naturally to me. I wanted to tell a story. In my therapeutic yoga private and group classes, I tell stories. I tell stories to inform, to help participants focus and keep them present, and I often tell stories to keep students in a posture for a lengthened amount of time. Yes, it's true, to distract them from the gentle "discomfort" of holding a posture for a long time.

This started back when I was a fitness instructor, leading basic step aerobic exercise with weights. Because I kept things simple, the process could be repetitive and a bit boring, so I told stories and gave information about the benefits of the work to the body to keep my students focused on something other than the burn that was happening in their arms, legs, and lungs.

So, in this book, to explain therapeutic yoga, doing so by telling a story just made sense to me. I wanted to create something that you could follow along with, something that was not too boring. I am a nerd at heart, and I can "geek out" on the science, physiology, and technical aspects of the therapeutic yoga practices that I have developed, but I realize that this could put everyone to sleep. So, stories it is.

It is my hope that this book and other future manuscripts will help deliver the approach that I created for self-care using therapeutic yoga to those who need it who are readers like me. I learned about and started my yoga lifestyle journey by reading books. I hope that you, and many others, will be inspired to begin your own personal journey with this book.

CHAPTER **1**

WHAT IS THERAPEUTIC YOGA?—THE PATH BECOMES THE METHOD

Therapeutic yoga is the term that I use to describe the practice that I developed over 40 years to help myself and others improve long-term health, functional mobility, and quality of life. This practice has a formal name, the Therapeutic Astanga Method©. This name more effectively describes the influences and origin of the practice that I developed, but it really doesn't mean much to anyone outside of the yoga world, and even then, the word "astanga" can be confused with a vigorous practice that was developed and shared by a well-known guru in India. This practice is not that, although both practices are using the physical postures of traditional Hatha yoga that have been shared by many teachers with their students over the past 150 years and subscribe to tenets of the same philosophy.

The Therapeutic Astanga Method©, that I call TAM© for ease, is my personal practice. I developed it in my living room over the course of many years. I had no intention of sharing it with anyone, of becoming a yoga teacher, of opening a yoga studio, of training yoga teachers, or of doing therapeutic yoga research. These things just happened because of the practice that I started in the '90s when I began to search for that thing that would help me move gracefully into and through the decades with vitality, balance, coordination, strength, and a sense of purpose.

TAM© has worked for me and the clients that I have served over the decades. I am sharing it with you because I know that it works. I have witnessed the beneficial results in myself and in the clients that had enough faith in me and the process to put the method into practice. I continue to do the research with my team that has confirmed the beneficial results in survivors of cancer who participated in the practices three times per week for four to six months. I am eternally

1

grateful for the opportunity to serve and to continue to share this method with as many people that are interested. I am happy to share it with you, the reader. I look forward to hearing about your experience with this practice.

As I mentioned earlier, I gave this method a name—Therapeutic Astanga Method© or TAM©. It was important to have a name that could identify and distinguish the practice when it came time to share it with aspiring yoga teachers and yoga students who wanted to deepen their practice in my continuing education and yoga teacher training workshops. The word "therapeutic" relates to the physical therapy practice that I was formally trained in. But that is about as far as the connection goes. Traditional Western physical therapy as it is often practiced in the United States is often dictated by the insurance industry, which likes to view a patient as individual parts, i.e., a knee problem, instead of a whole being that has a condition influenced by biological, psychological, and social conditions and paradigms.

I hope you will consider implementing a breath-centered therapeutic yoga practice into your daily living to benefit your long-term mobility, strength, flexibility, endurance, and mind/body/spirit well-being.

I AM AN EIGHT-LIMBED YOGA LIFESTYLE PRACTITIONER

When I started reading about and then eventually experienced the physical practices of yoga, I had no intention of sharing them with anyone. This was my personal exploration into a practice that I hoped might help me move through the decades with grace. I was not thinking about teaching yoga, and the idea of opening a yoga studio was not on my radar. I had discovered a passion for movement early in my life when I discovered exercise, dance, and movement practices in high school. It felt good to move, stretch, and strengthen my body. I realize now that this was the beginning of my learning how to settle my overactive nervous system and learning how to connect with myself.

I was able to share my passion for movement and exercise with others when I began to lead groups in high school. I was intrigued with the human body and how it functioned, how it got sick and then healed. I was naturally drawn to the medical profession and for a few years thought that I might go to medical school. As it turned out, my own journey with physical illness gave me opportunities to be in doctors' offices. I realized quickly that a physician might only spend five minutes with their patients. I felt that this was not enough time to make a positive impact in someone's life.

I began to investigate other professions and discovered physical therapy when I read about it in a college course manual. I didn't know anything about physical therapy. The manual said something to the effect that physical therapists help persons who have been injured, or are ill, to return to function by improving their strength with exercise or helping them to walk and recover from different ailments. I don't remember much else, but the idea that I could help people regain their life through exercise seemed like a natural progression from what I was doing already. I also noticed that physical therapists (at that time) could begin practicing with a bachelor's degree. That meant that I might begin my career after four years instead of the years that it might take to get through college, medical school, and residency. It made sense to my then younger self that I should try this. I applied and was accepted, not knowing anything about what I was getting into. This was a step in the right direction. I had no idea that there would be detours and roadblocks along the way.

During my college years, I had the opportunity to take dance, theater, computer, and movement classes along with my full course load of science classes that were preparing me for the physical therapy coursework. The melding of anatomy, physiology, technology, movement, and humanities coursework helped to set the foundation for the passion that was growing within me. I was able to lead group exercise and begin personal training in college as a fitness instructor. It was a natural bridge to expanding my passion for movement and helping others as I made my way into the physical therapy world.

Personal health challenges during that time made me acutely aware of the role that exercise and movement made in what I believed was just my physical health. I later discovered that my ailments were related to imbalance in both my mental and spiritual health. This insight would later help me to better understand the experiences of my clients, so it was a blessing. It just did not seem like a blessing at the time. Over time, I began to see a connection between health and longevity. I realized that my personal health was important and that I might be able to help others achieve better health over many years If I too could stay on the planet with a healthy body.

In these early years, I had gotten a glimpse of what some elders were able to accomplish in their lives and the lives of others when they kept their bodies mobile and strong. I saw a direct correlation with their mental acuity. I had survived physical therapy school, had become a physical therapist, and was still leading group fitness classes. In my time as a clinician and group fitness instructor—yes, as a 25-year-old—I had already witnessed and met some of the healthiest elders that I had ever known. They knew something that I didn't. I wanted to know what they knew. I wanted to be able to grow old with grace. I wanted to be able to move my body and help others for as long as possible. I knew that there was a way although I didn't know exactly what it was at the time. I was witnessing it in these healthy elders.

During those years, I was accessing the beginning tools that would eventually help me to create a unique approach using movement, breathwork, and awareness practices to encourage optimum long-term health and well-being. I had no idea that the most important learning tools would come from time spent reading, studying, and practicing yoga in my living room years later.

These things and more began my quest to find that "thing" that could help me move through the next decades with grace and possibly be the healthiest and most active elder that I could be.

CONTINUING MY EDUCATION

Many people read books for pleasure. Well, I like to read technical manuals for fun. I enjoy learning about how to do things and have learned how to do basic plumbing, as well as all sorts of other things by reading about it. Thirty years ago, I decided that I would read about yoga so that I could learn more about it. Eventually, I put the books down and began the physical practices. When I got the opportunity, I began studying with my teacher, Beryl Bender (also known as Beryl Bender Birch). This is when I began to realize that there was so much more to yoga than just the physical practice. I noticed a calm and stillness in her and that intrigued me. It was opposite of the way that I felt on most days at that time. I wanted to know more and decided to continue studying with Beryl. She introduced me to the Eight-Limbed Path as described by Patanjali in the *Yoga Sutras*, one of the foundational texts of classical yoga philosophy, during week-long yoga trainings over the course of many years.

At first, the group study sessions of the *Yoga Sutras* did not make any sense to me. I wanted to understand the theory behind the practices of the yoga lifestyle and couldn't help but want to know more about where this stuff came from. Over time, I found little nuggets of insight.

With much repetition, the content of the ancient readings in the *Yoga Sutras* began to unfold, and they began to get easier to understand.

What does all this have to do with the Eight Limbs? It is in the *Yoga Sutra* studies that I was first introduced to the concept of the Eight-Limbed Yoga Lifestyle or Path as described by Patanjali. These limbs are listed in Book Two, Verse 29 and then are expanded upon in more detail within different verses in the *Yoga Sutras*. Reading about these, studying, and sharing the ideas behind these verses repeatedly helped me make sense of them.

It began to dawn on me that the Eight Limbs felt familiar. I think it is because the first two limbs, called the "yamas" and the "niyamas," reminded me of the Ten Commandments. This was something that I had grown up with understanding, what I had considered to be as principles that I could follow to help me be the best human possible. These included, among other things, not harming, not hoarding, and not stealing—things I knew that were good principles to follow in life.

The third limb called "asana" was my favorite. Asana is the physical practice of yoga. Ah, exercise, yes, I could get into this. The fourth limb, "pranayama," which often translates to "breath control," made sense at the time. I mean, everyone must breathe. If you take the word "pranayama" apart it is made up of two words, "prana" and "ayama" in the Sanskrit language. The word "prana" is often defined as "life force" or "energy," and "ayama" is defined as control or restraint. The idea that "prana" could also mean "life force" or "energy" intrigued me. As a scientist, it made sense to me that everything is made up of energy, so there must be something behind this. As for the word "ayama," let me just say that I am a control freak that is living life in long-term recovery.

In the early days of my learning about the Eight-Limbed Path, I thought that practicing "pranayama" would make me a more efficient control freak. Boy, did I have that wrong. Now I recognize my desire to control things as one of the least healthy parts in my personality. This need for control prolongs my suffering when I am not able to control things around me, which is quite literally never. Thank goodness that I stuck with the practices. I still have a lot of work to do, but every day is a better day.

The fifth limb, "pratyahara," about sense withdrawal, was an interesting concept. It was not something that I was very familiar with, nor could I identify with it because I loved, almost craved sensual stimulation. I loved the taste of good food, the smell of the ocean, the sound of great music. The idea of withdrawing from sensual pleasure did not seem appealing to me. This tells you how little I knew about anything. I did not realize that my overstimulated sense awareness kept me in a torturous cycle overwhelmed with ideas or thoughts that made it difficult for me to concentrate and to find peace.

The sixth limb, "dharana," which is about focused concentration, was much harder for me to grasp. Looking back, I can understand why. This was a tough one for me at that time, and it still is. I was then, and can still be now, quite distractible. There is so much going on in the world that can make it hard to focus. I am slowly improving, but this one is real work.

The seventh limb, "dhyana," means "meditation." In the early stages of my practical experiences with yoga, this too seemed to be out of my reach. I was very hard on myself for failing at meditation. I did not realize back then that this yoga lifestyle practice was a process of evolution, that when I continued with my personal practices, that this too could and would change. Back then, I just decided to keep doing "pranayama" and "asana" (the breathing and the physical practices of yoga) and not force the meditation practice. I am glad that I did because my personal physical practice was exactly what I needed to help prepare me for the continuing adventures on my personal path of discovery in the yoga lifestyle practices. I am grateful.

"Samadhi," the eighth limb, has many definitions. Some define "samadhi" as the state where a yoga practitioner reaches spiritual enlightenment where the self, the mind, and the object of meditation merge together into one. Merriam-Webster defines "samadhi" as "a state of deep concentration resulting in union with or absorption into ultimate reality." I must admit that even though I consider myself a practitioner of the Eight-Limbed yoga lifestyle, I have little experience with this limb. As I have come to understand it, "samadhi" can be described as a state of bliss, or absolute union with the divine. I have a lot more work to do to even get close to achieving this. This is a state that I can only hope to achieve sometime in the next few lifetimes.

THE THERAPEUTIC ASTANGA METHOD©

What does all this have to do with the Therapeutic Astanga Method©? Over the course of years of studying and practicing yoga, working with my physical therapy patients and fitness clients, a process began to evolve. A process that I was using to guide my clients in the long-term care and maintenance of their whole self—mind, body, and spirit. The yoga lifestyle that I had been practicing, that involved the "asana," "pranayama," and attempts at "dhyana," was influencing the physical therapist and fitness practitioner in me. I did not plan to combine these experiences, it just happened. Once I stepped on the path of learning about the yoga lifestyle, I couldn't help but to be influenced by it. As my teacher Beryl would often say, "Once you look over the fence, it's hard not to know what is on the other side."

I liked what was happening to me in my yoga lifestyle adventures (as I like to call them). I was able to experience moments of mental calm, my body felt limber and strong, and I began to have small moments of awareness of my actions, kind of like watching myself on a video screen. I would notice when my ego would rise in my interactions with the world and/or others, and I could see myself responding in a manner that not only was unattractive, but also very irritating to me. I can only imagine how irritating that I was to others. Over time, I was able to recognize how my actions affected others and that there could be better ways. I appreciated this slow evolution of my personal awareness. It wasn't then and still is not now easy to have these moments of understanding. They are humbling, but I feel that they are important moments.

I was experiencing a process of physical, mental, and emotional self-discovery within my personal yoga lifestyle practices in my day-to-day practice as a physical therapist. At the same time, I was working with clients who were experiencing limitation in mobility, pain, and injury. I strongly believe that more people should have the opportunity to have these experiences of self-discovery. This is one of the many reasons that I invite and encourage others to begin walking on a path towards self-discovery, using breath-centered therapeutic yoga practices as a guide.

I wasn't exactly aware of it at the time, but a method was evolving from my past personal study that involved reading about and practicing a variety of methods in Eastern medicine, Tai Chi, Qi Gong, martial arts, yoga, Pilates, and other fitness approaches. This method that was combining some of the best parts of my years of experience in fitness, physical therapy, and yoga was beginning to take form. The Therapeutic Astanga Method© (TAM©) was emerging. I began to recognize that the therapeutic practices that I had created to help improve my own personal situation had great potential to positively influence others. I had used the practices for my own personal journey in moving towards balance in mind/body/spirit. This was not planned, it just happened.

In the early '90s, I was in full-time practice as a physical therapist and continued to lead at least one evening group fitness class per week. I really enjoyed the group aspect of fitness. I enjoyed leading others and sharing methods for improving cardiovascular conditioning, whole body strength and mobility, and infusing postural awareness, spinal mobility, and joint-protective methods into my unique style of guiding fitness. Leading high intensity group fitness and strength and aerobic dance classes was something that I knew. It was something that I was very comfortable with. This was a part-time gig that allowed me to get in some exercise, socialize with others, and have fun at the same time.

My experience goes back to when I first started. I was 15 years old, exercising, dancing, stretching, and guiding my peers at a local fitness gym and then as a leader in my high school dance team. I sought opportunities to continue to lead exercise on campus at college, then off campus in a variety of part-time jobs in fitness gyms. This was something that I knew I could do, loved to do, and was pretty good at.

THE BEGINNING OF A METHOD

The Therapeutic Astanga Method© is the name that I gave to the process that I developed over the course of 40 years. When I am training other professionals, you might hear me refer to it with the acronym TAM©, but most times I respond with therapeutic yoga when I am asked what kind of yoga I offer.

I melded my experiences in physical therapy, fitness, and yoga lifestyle practices to empower individuals and ease their progress towards long-term, improved well-being, in their minds, bodies, and spirits. This is the process that I have been sharing with my clients, patients, students, mentees, family, friends, professional peers, and the medical and research communities that I have served over the years, all the while working to make the practice accessible to many.

Orthopedics, neurological, spine care, and pelvic health have been my specialties in the clinical work that I have done in my professional physical therapy practice. I have also had a special interest in elder care—or to be more precise, how to encourage humans to improve their long-term well-being into their later years. I have had the opportunity to run physical therapy clinics in the traditional way. I thoroughly enjoyed patient care as a program director in the outpatient world. Dealing with insurance companies, arguing with non-clinicians about what was "medically necessary" for my patients' care was one of my least favorite things to do. It was an important part of my work because my patients' physical therapy costs would not be covered by their insurance companies that were charging them excessive premiums for so-called "coverage." I realized early in my professional life that it was more appropriate to refer to the traditional "health care" in the United States as "sick care." Preventative services were rarely, if ever, covered, leading to heated discussions with insurance case managers. It seemed that patients were only referred to physical therapy when their conditions had progressed to a state of incredible pain and dysfunction.

Despite the daily challenge of dealing with the traditional insurance system, the thing that kept me eager to return to my job on a day-to-day basis was that I thoroughly enjoyed the process of being in direct patient care. It was very rewarding to witness my patients' progress when they participated in physical therapy practices that improved their range of motion, strength, and endurance, and often, even their ability to walk without pain. Helping my patients to reduce their pain perception, so they could increase their activity level, and guiding them towards understanding that their personal commitment to a regular set of activities and exercise could help them find success in meeting their goals towards independence and a pain-free life. This process of direct patient care that I provided was all performed on a one-physical-therapist-to-one-patient basis in the physical therapy clinic. This was back in the early '90s. Our medical care system has changed a lot since then. Things are quite different now.

PHYSICAL THERAPIST BY DAY— FITNESS INSTRUCTOR BY EARLY EVENING

During the time that I held a day job as a physical therapist, I was still leading group fitness at least one evening a week at a local fitness gym. I enjoyed the group interaction and the ability to influence a whole group of people towards improved cardiovascular and strength fitness. It was like the work that I did as a physical therapist, yet different somehow. I was able to express myself in a different way and in a sense was able to deliver preventative health care to groups of like-minded individuals who were invested in their health. These clients were relatively healthy, and they each had a desire to improve their self-care skills and long-term well-being. This "work" did not involve any major paperwork, no arguing with insurance adjusters or case managers. It was rewarding in a very special way. I was supporting clients and offering preventative services to them while I was socializing and continuing to move my body on a regular basis, which I really enjoyed. I was meeting with, guiding, and exercising with groups of people that I might meet for the first time and then get to know quite well over months and years. I was able to form a bond of trust that resulted in lasting relationships and long-term friendships that I still have over 20 years later.

INTEGRATING PHYSICAL THERAPY, FITNESS, AND TRADITIONAL HATHA YOGA

In the time that I was practicing as a physical therapist and leading group fitness classes, I noticed that a large gap existed between the traditional outpatient physical therapy world and the traditional gym/exercise environment. When a patient had met their goals and completed their physical therapy treatment program, they were discharged from care and instructed to continue their individual home program on their own. Because I functioned in these two settings, I had the opportunity to witness the challenges that people experienced navigating between these two completely different environments. In the physical therapy clinic, a patient who had experienced illness or injury was under the direct care and supervision of a licensed physical therapist who would implement and direct their treatment program. In the "real world" of fitness, these patients were expected to continue their home program or begin a fitness routine on their own without specific direction or support, unless they hired a fitness trainer and not everyone had that option.

Another challenge that made the transition for physical therapy patients into the real world of fitness difficult was related to physical therapists not being allowed to treat the "whole person." Physical therapists functioning in the traditional medical system back then were constrained to treatments that were specific to the "body part" that was injured or in need of care. Insurance reimbursements would not cover activities that involved other areas of the body that were connected to the injured area. This is often still the case today. I had a real problem with that back then, as I do now.

I still disagree with the compartmentalization of human bodies in medical care, which involves treating persons who are experiencing an injury, illness, limitation, or medical condition as a "diagnosis" or injured body part, and not as a whole human being with a complex myriad of processes that are contributing to their dysfunction. I knew then, as I do now, that the body systems work in relation to each other part and that the most effective way to treat an injury or illness is through a whole-person approach. When I started to study and practice yoga, I realized that this was the whole mind, body, and spirit approach that I was looking for to meet my own personal long-term mental, physical, and spiritual health needs. The physical therapy clinical care that I provided always involved the whole person, and that was why I spent so much time arguing with medical insurance providers on the phone, advocating for my patients' long-term needs. It was just a matter of time before my personal exploration of the yoga lifestyle approaches began to influence my professional work.

In the clinic, we were limited in the amount of time and number of visits that we were allowed, or shall I say, that were covered and reimbursed for a typical injury or diagnosis. This made it important to be efficient and to do the best work that we could do in the time that we had with each patient. We did this out of respect for our patients' financial budgets too. This solidified the importance of developing an effective home exercise program that the patient would perform when they were not in the physical therapy clinic. It also helped them to develop their strength and endurance and to prepare for the next visit. I noticed that all patients did not always seem excited about doing their home exercise program. Some would report that they were doing their program, but it was obvious that they were falling short somewhere. In the days before my husband and I had our own family, I found it hard to understand what could possibly be preventing my physical therapy patients from performing their home program. Having kids gave me a whole new perspective about the challenge of practicing self-care and trying to achieve balance in work and family life.

In my physical therapy practice, I also had the privilege of working with patients who recognized the value of the homework that they were doing that was leading them back to health. It was these patients that I noticed who would ask about what the next step was when they completed physical therapy. I got questions about how they might be able to now go to their local fitness gym and continue their work towards improved health. Thinking about it now, I know that many of these patients also had been working on balancing work and family life. And yet, there was a difference in their motivation.

Meanwhile, at the fitness gyms where I led group exercise, I was being asked questions about how to participate in exercise and how to use the equipment in the gym more effectively after they had completed their physical therapy. I also heard these questions from persons who had a previous history of orthopedic, spine, or neurological injury, who may not have had recent physical therapy and wanted to know how to participate in a program and not reinjure themselves in the process.

Occasionally, I would hear a group fitness client say to me, "I haven't been in class for three months because I had an injury and was in physical therapy, and now I am back in the gym. My doctor and my physical therapist say that I am cleared to return to exercise in the gym, but I don't know where to begin." I noticed that there was a very wide gap between the movement and exercises that physical therapy patients were guided in and the activities that were available in a traditional gym environment. Physical therapy treatment programs consisted of conservative and careful activities that were appropriate for the initial stage of rehabilitating an injury. They did not resemble typical gym activities.

As physical therapists, we had to be creative in scheduling our patients' treatment sessions to give them time to heal and to help maximize the benefit from the program that we were developing. The home exercise program was very important because patients were often limited in the number of visits that they received for these treatments. Their work at home expanded the treatment program. Once those visits were over, as physical therapists, we would re-evaluate and either renegotiate with the insurance company and/or request backup from the patients' referring physicians to be able to continue helping patients. When the patient had met the goals that were set for the treatment, they were discharged from physical therapy. This is where some patients found themselves being let loose in the "wild west" of the fitness gym. It made for an almost impossible hurdle, their having to negotiate between the conservative approach in their structured physical therapy treatment program and the "good luck doing this on your own" fitness gym environment.

I noticed that most of the people who experienced physical therapy for rehabilitation of an injury often tried but failed at successfully transitioning to continue their exercise in the fitness gym. Eventually, they stopped being active, and that kept them in a continuous cycle of pain and dysfunction, that led them back to physical therapy, which would provide improvement in function and reduced pain. They would get discharged, fail to maintain a consistent long-term fitness program, and eventually return to physical therapy, or worse, they might stop trying and just decide to live with the pain. It was difficult to witness this, but I knew that there were many processes in motion that were outside of my control. Stress has a way of manifesting itself into tension and pain in many parts of the body, and there is often so much more that is going on in a person's life that puts them at greater risk of experiencing pain and dysfunction. I had experienced this myself and had witnessed it in my clients so often that it became apparent that there was an opportunity for me to use my unique skills to help this specific niche of clients. This is how I slowly began to make my move into the integrative world of therapeutic yoga and wellness that I exist in now.

CHAPTER 2

WHO YOU MEET CAN CHANGE YOUR LIFE—THE FIRST SESSION

C aroline had a problem. Her back would go into full spasm, and when it did, the pain was so intense that it would leave her unable to function fully in her daily life for weeks at a time. It started with minor episodes of pain in her low back and hip that would last for a few days. Over 10 years, the episodes got more intense, lasted longer, and began to occur more frequently. She was tired and scared that the pain would return and that one day it might not ever go away. She worried that surgery might be her only option but recalled her mother having had a failed surgical procedure that had left her incapacitated, in pain, and permanently disabled. She wondered if she was destined to the same fate.

Caroline was beginning to lose hope when she met one of my long-term clients. They struck up a casual conversation that eventually turned to their shared history of back pain and the impact that it had on their ability to live their lives to the fullest. My client shared the success she had using therapeutic yoga to improve her mobility and strength and recommended that Caroline call me for advice. She had never heard about therapeutic yoga but was willing to make the call. She believed that she had nothing to lose by reaching out to get information.

Caroline took a chance, made the call, scheduled an assessment, and made a commitment to do the work. In the process, she learned how to take care of her whole self, mind, body, and spirit, by incorporating therapeutic yoga into her everyday wellness practice. This is the story of our time together, the development and then gradual progression and implementation of Caroline's therapeutic yoga program, and the work that she did that improved her long-term well-being and changed her function and quality of life for the better.

I am sharing the process of our sessions. I am sharing the practices that Caroline experienced that were designed to help her step forward on the path of mindful and breath-centered awareness as she improved the stability of her spine and mobility of her body, or—as she called it—eliminated her back pain.

As an integrative physical therapist and therapeutic yoga specialist, I have had the privilege of working with many different people over the years, helping them to discover the tools that lie within themselves by implementing the Therapeutic Astanga Method© to help them move away from pain and dysfunction and towards improved physical functioning, well-being, and quality of life for the long term. Caroline was one of these people. I am grateful for the opportunity that I had to share the therapeutic yoga practices that I developed over the course of 40 years, melding my experience in physical therapy, fitness, and yoga to create my interpretation of therapeutic yoga. This method is one tool, among a host of many varied approaches, that can be used by an individual to help them move away from pain and dysfunction. Because of the complex nature of pain and its origins, I do not consider it a "cure-all," but I believe it is a good place to begin.

Caroline was willing to do just that. To begin on a new path of action by using the personalized therapeutic yoga practices to help her move away from pain and dysfunction and move forward to living her best life beyond her retirement. I am grateful that she had faith in me and the therapeutic yoga practices, but more importantly that she had faith in herself. She did the work and reaped the rewards of her consistent effort.

THERAPEUTIC YOGA WORKS

I know that therapeutic yoga works because I have been developing breath-centered mindful awareness practices over the last few decades and have shared these programs that have made a positive impact in the lives of my clients, yoga students, and small groups since I began offering them in the late '90s.

The term "therapeutic yoga" is not always well understood. There is a common misconception that all yoga is therapeutic, and I believe that all yoga should be therapeutic. Unfortunately, this is not always the case. Just like any other wellness practice that can involve movement, it can be treated like exercise without attention to maintaining a mindful approach. This statement opens up a discussion that is beyond the scope of the information that I will be presenting in my writing.

Therapeutic yoga has often been referred to as the application of yoga postures and lifestyle practices directed to the treatment of health conditions that involves instruction in yogic practices. These practices are put into action to prevent, reduce, or alleviate structural, physiological, emotional, and spiritual pain, suffering, or limitations. I created a unique approach to the development and delivery of therapeutic yoga programs when I began to combine my experiences as a physical therapist, fitness instructor, and yoga practitioner. I was able to personally experience the benefits of regularly practicing therapeutic yoga, which include improved muscular strength and body flexibility, improved respiratory function, improved cardiovascular function, reduced stress, reduced anxiety, reduced depression, reduced chronic pain, improved sleep patterns, and enhanced overall well-being and quality of life. These benefits and more are why I am moved to share therapeutic yoga with others and why I am writing this book.

If you are suffering from back pain, spasm, instability, and dysfunction, I hope that you will continue reading and then consider exploring the gentle breath-centered therapeutic yoga practices that I am sharing in this book. I want to be clear that these mindful physical practices are not meant to be considered the only approach available, since each person living with pain will come to the practice with their own individual experience. These practices are meant to complement all sorts of therapeutic interventions and are designed to empower the user towards achieving their best outcome. I have developed these therapeutic yoga practices to be an entry point for those who are ready to step on the path towards freedom from many of the limitations that living with pain can bring. In this book, you will discover that I am sharing the most effective gentle therapeutic yoga practices that had the greatest positive impact on the core stability, functional mobility, and overall well-being of my clients with back pain over the last few decades. I created these practices for myself to improve my own long-term health, spine mobility, strength, and well-being. I share them with as many people as are interested via private, small group, and professional speaking and conference engagements. I hope that you will learn how to use these practices to help you move towards balance and possibly away from pain and dysfunction. In case you aren't sure, I want to let you know that when you do therapeutic yoga—the ONLY thing that you have to do is BREATHE—and the rest will fall into place with gentle and consistent effort. Get started on the path by reading this book.

GETTING TO KNOW CAROLINE

Over 35 years Caroline had made a comfortable life for herself in the real estate market along with her husband and was recently retired. She was at the stage in her life where her grown children had begun their independent lives and started families of their own. Being a grandmother was unfamiliar territory, but she was excited for this next phase of her life that included spending time with her husband traveling, visiting with family and friends, and finally having time for herself. She was a woman whom you felt a distinct connection with as soon as you met her. There was a soft kindness in the way that she spoke that made you feel that you had been friends for years. She was smart and creative with a wry sense of humor that snuck up on you if you weren't fully attentive.

I will never forget our first phone conversation where Caroline said, "I met a woman on a shopping trip. She said that I need to call you about my back pain." She continued to share that they had struck up a conversation where Caroline had mentioned her history of back pain over the last 20 years that had progressed significantly in the last seven. "I was so happy to be going on this trip because I had not traveled at all that year. I was eager to get out of the house." She went on to explain that she had a history of back trouble that, when she had a flare-up, left her unable to function fully because of debilitating pain and spasm.

She paused, "When it first started, it only lasted a few days and happened once a year. As the years have passed, these episodes have become more frequent and are lasting longer each time." She went on to share that in the last 12 months, each episode lasted three months. "When I went on that trip, I was so happy to finally be out of the house with less pain because in the year before that trip, my back 'went out' three times."

Her voice hardened when she shared that she was tired and frustrated that this was happening so often now. She mentioned that she had tried traditional physical therapy for a few weeks in the past, but because she was working full-time then, she had not been consistent with her appointments. "I didn't do the exercises that they gave me. I didn't have time. Well, I guess that I did not make the time to do them." She sighed and asked, "Can you help me?"

I responded, "Let's look at our schedules, set an appointment to meet, and see what's going on in your body."

We agreed on a date and time to meet, and I said, "Caroline, I want to be very clear. This appointment is part me evaluating your situation to see if there is something that I can offer you to help your current state of being. The other part is that during this appointment, you will have the opportunity to determine if you want me to be on your long-term health and wellness team. During our session, we'll get to know each other better and expand upon this initial phone conversation. I'll guide you through some activities, look at your posture, assess your breathing, and watch you move. We'll work on getting down on the floor and getting back up."

She sucked in her breath and said with a note of concern in her voice, "I can't remember the last time that I was on the floor. I just remember the last time my back went out. I was sitting at my desk and reached over to pick up some mail that had fallen on the floor and—BOOM." She fell silent.

I continued, "We will move forward, depending upon what we find on our first session. You are not reporting active symptoms at this time, but if your situation warrants it, I'll recommend that I provide physical therapy care, and we'll connect with your medical team, develop a plan of care, and implement it to help you move forward. Your situation sounds chronic, and if the results of my assessment confirm this, then I'll develop a gentle therapeutic yoga program based on our findings. I'll then begin to guide you in the therapeutic yoga practices that will get you started back on the road to wellness. This is going to take commitment and consistent effort."

Caroline said, "I am so ready. I have got to do this. I'm at a different place in my life. I have these grandbabies now, I want to spend time with them, and I don't know what I'll do if this pain comes back. My doctors say that I have some bone spurs and a slight bulge in my lower spine, but I don't need surgery—yet. I just want to get my life back. I'm willing to do the work."

We agreed that it was worth trying, and we set our first appointment for a therapeutic yoga/physical therapy consultation. This was back in the days before I opened my first commercial studio location, when I was still doing private work on site at my clients' homes.

WEEK ONE: THE FIRST SESSION

It was a lovely fall afternoon in the outskirts of the hill country in Texas on the first day that I drove to Caroline's home for our initial consultation. The air was crisp and dry, the sun was shining, and the leaves were green on the live oak trees that dotted the landscape. Mornings might be 50 degrees, but as soon as the sun peeked out, we might see a beautiful 80-degree day emerge, so you had to dress ready for the change. I had lived in the area for a while and was ready for it.

The drive through Caroline's neighborhood was pleasant. She had built a home with her husband on a five-acre tract of land. It was peaceful and quiet with the sound of birds chirping when I stepped up to the front door to ring the bell.

Caroline greeted me warmly as she opened the door. She was dressed in coordinated warm-up pants and a top with sneakers. She led me into a moderate-sized fitness room that had a padded floor, treadmill, recumbent bicycle, mirrored walls, a weight bench, barbells, and free weights.

I commented, "It looks like you have a great space to do your practice. Have you been using the treadmill or stationary cycle for exercise? This equipment could be a great addition to your program."

"Oh, this is my husband's workout space. I haven't ever used this equipment. I didn't think I could with my back problems."

I shared that we would be using the space for her practice, and depending on the results of our assessment that day, we would decide what equipment that she might benefit from using, if any. I asked her if we might find a place to sit comfortably for the beginning of our session where we would complete our initial intake questionnaire and documents related to our contract agreements. She led me to the living room, and we sat down for our conversation.

I guided Caroline through what I now refer to as the Therapeutic Yoga Assessment. This is where we continued with the conversation that we'd started over the phone to expand my awareness of her medical and activity history and get more information about her then current situation. We started with a review of an intake questionnaire that she had filled out prior to our meeting.

Caroline had a history of back pain that had started in her mid-thirties. She reported that she had been in a car accident in her twenties but had not sustained any major injuries at that time, just soreness. She reported that she had always led an active lifestyle that included occasional family ski trips, hiking, and some group fitness classes. She discovered running in her thirties and was able to keep her fitness by running daily, early in the morning before her family and work responsibilities began. She added, "I must admit, I am not a flexible person, and I never enjoyed stretching, so I never did it. I hope therapeutic yoga can help me."

A common statement that I get from people that I meet who learn about my profession is "You teach yoga classes? I can't do yoga. I am not flexible." A common myth that surrounds yoga is that you must be flexible to do it. I often share that the therapeutic yoga practices that I develop are not only about flexibility; instead, they involve the process of utilizing awareness practices that include developing mobility within the body, which is a combination of strength and flexibility. That the practices are designed to help persons meet their individual needs and to improve their long-term well-being.

"I am concerned about my back. Do you think I will need surgery?" she asked as she handed me several sheets of paper that contained the results of X-ray and MRI scans that she had taken in the last two years. I reviewed the results that showed some bony spurs at the lumbar spine and a slight posterior and lateral bulge to the right side at the lumbar 4 and 5 levels of the spine. "Do you think that this is what is causing my pain?" she asked.

I responded, "It is not uncommon for a person in their late fifties to have changes in their spine like the ones that you are demonstrating. The longer that we are on the planet, and depending on our activity level, the chances increase that we will see some changes in the back, or as I prefer to identify it—the spine. These types of changes do not always determine the cause of pain. In fact, there are research studies that have been done on the spine of persons who demonstrated similar changes, and they had no pain. In other situations, patients had significant back pain and no disc or bony changes. The cause of back pain and spine dysfunction are complex and can even go beyond challenges to the physical body to include psychological trauma. We are still learning about the causes of and the experience for people who are living with back pain."

Caroline's brow furrowed, and the look on her face seemed as if she was searching for words when she said, "That doesn't help me much."

I took in a slow breath to give her some time to continue with her thoughts. She maintained the focused expression on her face for a minute before her expression brightened, and she exclaimed. "Well, if this is the case, maybe my pain is not related to what the MRIs and the scans say. Maybe there is hope for me after all."

I let out a sigh of relief.

This was an important moment for the communication between us to be very clear. I believe that my clients are benefited greatly by knowing as much as they want to know about how their body functions, and when possible, to help them understand the source of their dysfunction when it is present. I want to be able to address and answer, if possible, all the questions that my clients have about their potential for improvement based on the current assessment of their condition. I let my clients know that if they ask me a question, I will answer directly to the best of my ability. If I can't answer their question, I will check with my network to see if we can find an answer.

I continued and shared that our work on that day would be focused on finding any relationship to the source of her past spine pain challenges. Our conversation progressed with more questions about her history, and then I asked her about any goals that she had for the short and long term.

You may have noticed that I have been referring to the "back" as the "spine." I want you to know that I prefer to use the term "spine" when it relates to the physiology of the body because I find that I can be more specific in communicating with my clients when I use that term. Yes, I am an anatomy nerd, and old habits die hard since I have been functioning as an integrative spine specialist for a long time. I have spent much of my professional life navigating between two worlds, the yoga and fitness communities of health-minded people where everyone uses recognizable words to describe general concepts of the body in motion. Then there's the physical therapy, science, and research world where my peers often use more technical language to describe very specific processes or situations.

I am challenged because the term "back pain" can be general, and if there is a problem in the "back," this does not tell me much about where I can expect the problem to be. I often hear people talk about their back pain when they are pointing to their hip or to a general area along their rib cage. I use the word "spine" to help me to be more specific when communicating with my clients, patients, therapeutic yoga students, and my professional peers, of course. I do a lot of teaching with my clients during our sessions, bringing out images or models of the spine. It is in these sessions that I review the parts of the spine and nervous system so that my clients can learn where the cervical (neck), thoracic (rib cage), lumbar (low back), or sacral (pelvic/tail bone) areas are located.

At the end of the day, I use the term "spine" because it just makes sense to me and I want to help others learn as much as they care to know about how their body functions and what its parts are called, so that they can, in turn, communicate more effectively with their medical and health care providers. I am not trying to be fancy or sound like a science snob, nor am I saying that it is wrong to use the word "back." I am just more comfortable with "spine." You can expect that I will most often be using the word "spine" in the rest of this book.

Caroline's eyes moistened when she shared, "Our youngest son is getting married next year. I would really like to be able to help him and his fiancée with the wedding preparations and want to attend the wedding feeling strong. More important than whether I can function, I must look good in my outfit." She broke the serious tone, and we laughed.

I continued, "Well, that is an excellent goal to work towards. Looking good and feeling strong. You've already started this trend by wearing a coordinated outfit for this session. Thank you for sharing this important goal with me."

She smiled, and we moved into the fitness room, where I asked her to remove her shoes.

Caroline said in a surprised tone, "I have to show you my feet?"

I replied, "Yes, Caroline. I prefer that we do the practices in bare feet. It allows me and you to see how well your feet are connecting to the earth and tells me a lot about the foundation of stability that you are starting this practice with. I also will be able to help guide you in activities to help in case we find something lacking."

Caroline was listening to me while she sat down on a bench in the room and removed her sneakers and socks. She laughed when she said, "I am glad that I did my pedicure last week."

I told her that I have seen some interesting looking feet over the years, beginning with my own, that her feet looked just fine and that she could be proud. I placed a yoga mat on the floor, and we began our work.

Dear readers, please note that in Chapter 11 "Therapeutic Yoga Practice," you will find images of this posture as well as all yoga postures given in this book. The image of mountain pose appears on page 138. As a reminder, if you'd like a hard copy of the images and descriptions of the therapeutic yoga poses presented in this book, go to my website TherapeuticYogaWorks.com to find the PDF to print out.

We begin in standing mountain pose, feet parallel and hip distance* apart.

[Close your mouth, and breathe gently through your nose. Begin in the standing position in the standing mountain pose with your eyes open. Look forward, and place your gaze on a point ahead of you that is not moving. Position your feet parallel and hip distance apart. Feel the weight even between the ball of the foot and the heel of the foot. Even between the right and left foot. Breathe.

Bring your awareness to your toes. Gently lift the toes while keeping the ball of your feet grounded to the mat to encourage the support of the muscular arch in each foot. Breathe.

Bring your attention to your knees. Activate the muscles in your lower body by creating a microscopic bend in both knees. Just enough to feel the support of the muscles in the front and back of your knees. Breathe.

Bring your attention to the position of your hips and spine. Feel your body weight settling evenly between the right and left hip. Feel a sense of elongation along your spine. Allow these areas to be positioned comfortably as you stand. Feel the gentle movement of your breath that influences your torso as you stand tall. Draw your shoulders gently back towards your spine and then down towards your pelvis. Feel the sensation of lengthening along the side of your neck as the shoulders move down and away from your ears. Breathe.

Feel an energetic lengthening of the arms that are resting alongside your body. Feel the energy moving through the arms all the way down to your fingertips. Feel the connection of your feet to the earth, and begin to visualize your energetic life force combining with that of the earth, and follow this force as it moves upward through the lower legs, thighs, through your hips and torso, along your spine, and upwards all the way to the top of your head. Feel your whole body simultaneously energized and calm. Stand tall in this position for 10 breaths. Fully aware of your surroundings and fully aware of maintaining smooth, gentle, and rhythmic breathing.]

Standing mountain is a posture that many yoga practitioners can begin to take for granted because it does not look as impressive compared to other standing yoga postures. In my experience it is a fundamental posture that is important because the foundation of this posture exists in and will influence every other posture that the practitioner attempts in their personal gentle therapeutic yoga practice. The standing mountain posture provides information about a client's awareness of their body's position in space and their standing postural habits. It can show restrictions that could nega-tively influence major joints in the body. This posture also provides a snapshot of the client's beginning point in their program.

Even though the standing mountain posture does not look very complicated, it is not as easy as one might think. It requires the prac-titioner to stand upright with awareness in a balanced and ready state of attention while maintaining smooth and rhythmic breath-ing. I often have clients begin the practice of standing mountain posture while lying on their backs at the beginning stages of their therapeutic yoga program. This helps the client rest with support on the firm surface of the mat on the floor and can help provide them feedback regarding their body position as they work towards bringing their alignment into balance.

*Hip distance apart is a reference point of alignment that I like to use to help place the thighs in as close to a neutral position as pos-sible. It can be determined and identified as the position of aligning the feet in the same distance apart as the distance that lies between the place where the thigh bone inserts into the pelvic bone. I am not referring to aligning the feet as wide as the outside of the hips.

We started in the standing mountain posture to help Caroline begin to bring awareness to her breath and body while she was stand-ing. "Take a moment to feel the sensation of your feet connecting with the mat while you breathe through your nose, mouth closed." Caroline stood still, listening to every word. I began to guide her through the Therapeutic Sun Salutation©. I noticed that she hesitat-ed when asked to do the standing variation of the cat/cow posture. As if her body wasn't sure what to do.

Getting down to the floor was slow, but she was able to get into a downward-facing dog, and I saw her tense up. "Keep breathing," I said. I had noticed Caroline holding her breath during the motion when she was trying to move to the floor and maintain the down-ward-facing dog. She took a long breath and was able to get down onto her hands and knees, and then she moved slowly as I guided her to move onto her back with her knees bent.

"Wow, that was harder than I expected, my arms were shaking, and I'm perspiring. Who knew that this could be so hard?"

I shared with her that her body was out of practice, but with a few sessions, it would likely realize that this was an important practice and would get "on board" with the program.

"I didn't realize how out of shape I am right now. I used to be so active. Is there any hope for me?"

I told her, "I'm sure that your body is surprised by our actions right now, but let's give it a few days. With a little practice, I believe that your body might decide that what we are doing together here is a good thing."

I asked Caroline to be kind in her thoughts about her body because it was listening, or shall I say, that her nervous system was paying attention. I shared that what we think in our minds influences our body's ability to perform and participate in challenging activities ("upanishads"). That, if we believe that we can do something, then our nervous system follows along until it is proven wrong. Often, we just must begin the process. I recommended that we start slow and that we be consistent. "Let's allow your nervous system to recognize this work as a good thing."

Caroline asked, "Are you sure that my older body will buy into this? It's been a long time since I really did any form of exercise."

I shared that there was nothing to lose and much to gain by trying.

She conceded, "Okay, we've just met. You talk a good game and come highly recommended, so I trust you. I'm willing to try."

The Therapeutic Sun Salutation©

This is a movement sequence that I developed to help my clients get down on to the floor and get up off the floor. I get a lot of information about a person's abilities and limitations when I guide them through this activity. This movement sequence also helps to address the often-unspoken topic of the risk of falls that could change the course of a person's independence and long-term health. This is as good a time as any for you to try this. You can find images of this sequence in Chapter 11 on page 135.

[Begin in standing mountain posture with your hands at heart center, your feet parallel and hip distance apart. Check in to feel the weight even between both feet and keep the weight even between the ball of the foot and the heel on both sides. Lift your toes to begin to engage the muscles that support the structural arch in your feet. Then stretch the toes and relax them to rest on the mat.

During this and every activity, do the best that you can to breathe through your nose with your mouth closed. Do the best that you can.

Practicing Gratitude: Focus your attention on something that you are grateful for today.

Inhale: Reach your arms out to the side and over your head.

Exhale: Bring your hands down and back to your heart.

Repeat three times.

"Inhale, reach up, exhale, hands to heart."

Inhale: Reach your arms out to the side and over your head.

Exhale: Bring your hands down and back to your heart while you bend your knees and sit your bottom back as if moving to sit into a chair.

Inhale: Straighten the legs as you reach your arms out to the side and over your head.

Exhale: Bring your hands down and back to your heart while you bend your knees and sit your bottom back as if moving to sit into a chair.

Repeat three times.

Inhale: Reach up.

Exhale: Bring the hands to the thighs.

Repeat three times.

Inhale: Reach up.

Exhale: Bring the hands to the thighs, and hold them there.

Stay in the knees bent with your spine in neutral position.

Prepare to move the spine.

Inhale: Extend the spine.

Exhale: Flex and round through the spine.

Repeat three times.

Inhale: Sweep your arms out to the sides and overhead while you straighten your knees to come back to upright standing.

Exhale: Bring your hands to your heart center to return to standing mountain.

Now widen the stance by stepping the feet wider than hip distance apart. Keep your knees and feet parallel, and keep the weight even between the ball of the feet and the heels on each foot.

Inhale: Reach up.

Exhale: Bend the hips, bend the knees, and drop your bottom as low as it feels comfortable (hands to thighs).

Repeat three times.

If it feels right, sit your bottom back, and touch the mat with your hands.

Inhale: Reach up and—if you can—touch the mat.

Exhale: Let's do it again.

Inhale: Reach up.

Exhale: Bring your hands down, and touch the mat.

Push your strong arms and hands into the mat.

Walk your feet back into the downward-facing dog.

The fingers are wide, the head is relaxed. Push yourself away from the floor. Don't worry if the heels are not touching the mat.

Breathe! Three breaths here.

From this position bend the knees to bring them down the mat, and sit your bottom back into child's pose. Breathe!]

I get a lot of information from my clients when I take them through the Therapeutic Sun Salutation©. When I am guiding the client through the movements, I can assess their whole-body mobility, flexibility, and functional strength. I can observe their breathing patterns during the basic—and for some, often challenging—activities involved in getting down to and then up from the floor with awareness. The Therapeutic Sun Salutation© is a movement sequence that I developed as the result of my personal experience combining physical therapy, fitness, and traditional Hatha yoga movement practices. I developed a variation of the traditional Sun Salutation A that I had been using in my own personal practice when I noticed that it was not accessible to many, especially those individuals who were living with back pain. I am very happy to share the variation that I created. I especially love the Therapeutic Sun Salutation© practice because once the client learns how to use it, they can reduce their risk of being stuck on the floor in the event of an accidental fall, and they can also use it to check in with their body, to do a self-assessment of how well their body is moving and functioning in the moment.

The time that we spent in conversation directly after Caroline had successfully moved from the Therapeutic Sun Salutation© activity down to the floor to lie on her back was no accident. This was time that I spent observing her ability to recover from the movements that she had just experienced. If she had reported a history of cardiac problems, I would have taken blood pressure and pulse at the beginning of our intake conversation and then at different points during the assessment. This would have been one of those points. Since she did not have this history, I used observation of her breath and any holding patterns that she might have used during the movements to the floor and how long it took her to come back to a rested state after the exertion.

By the end of our discussion and the end of her performing the Therapeutic Sun Salutation©, I knew that Caroline was an excellent candidate for a therapeutic yoga practice that I could develop and guide her through using the Therapeutic Astanga Method©. It would be just one of the many tools that she could use to help her alleviate pain and return to a higher level of physical functioning.

I want to be clear when I state that at this point, I can see the physical challenges that Caroline's pain has brought to her, but it doesn't mean that I believe that her pain is necessarily purely physical in origin. Pain is a very complex process, and we are just beginning to scratch the surface in our understanding of the many ways that pain manifests itself in people. There are many things that can be at the root cause for someone who is living with pain. Some of those things include past physical or emotional trauma, neurological changes, psychological challenges, anxiety, depression, and/or stress. That is just a short list, and I know that I couldn't list every potential process that might be at the root cause of a client's pain.

The therapeutic yoga practices that I offer are designed to empower my clients in their practice of self-care activities that help them to begin to settle their nervous system. They learn how to use the attention to their breath as a focal point during gentle movements to help encourage the nervous system to begin to trust the movement practices that can eventually lead to improved strength and range of motion within the body. The gentle and consistent effort produced during the therapeutic yoga practice can allow the relaxation response to take over and potentially reduce the sensation of pain and the limitation that can come from it.

Where was I? Oh yes. Caroline was a great candidate for therapeutic yoga because she was not showing signs of an acute pain episode that needed physical therapy or collaboration with her medical team and because she expressed enthusiasm and readiness to "do the work" to improve her function and be free from pain. I often request that my clients share with their medical providers that they are participating in therapeutic yoga under my supervision. This helps the client's physician and other medical specialists know what their patient is up to and helps me to make sure that the therapeutic yoga program is not conflicting with other treatment approaches. This also allows the medical team to ask any questions that they might have regarding the process that their patient will be experiencing. This open communication is very good for my client, and it also helps to increase awareness of the specialized integrative therapeutic yoga practices that I have developed and am providing as a service within our community. Calls, emails, or texts from my clients' physicians often open the door for future referrals. This has helped me to build my referral network and gain clients over the years. I am particularly interested in medical specialists who are open to conservative and integrative management for their patients.

THE MOST IMPORTANT THING THAT YOU WILL DO TODAY IS BREATHE

I asked Caroline if she was comfortable lying on her back. Because she said she felt fine, I began to guide her into a beginning awareness practice of three-part diaphragmatic breathing. It goes like this, so if you are reading this and want to try it, keep reading and follow along. If you are listening to this, even better; just follow along. If all else fails, you can access and download the PDF to this and the practices within this book on my website at TherapeuticYogaWorks.com.

Breathe to reduce stress, mobilize your body, and activate the relaxation response.

1. Take a moment to settle into a comfortable position, either sitting or lying down.
2. Close your mouth, and bring your attention to your breath as it moves gently in and out of your nose. Breathe in, breathe out.
3. Focus your attention on your body as you rest. Allow your whole body to drop into the surface that supports you, and let go of any tension that you might be holding. Allow yourself to feel the softness that exists in your body. Breathe in, breathe out.
4. Bring your attention to the softness of your abdomen, the throat, the front of your torso and your pelvic floor. Allow these areas to move gently as you breathe. Notice the gentle expansion as you inhale and the gentle release inward as you exhale. Let your breath move you. There is no need to force or push. Breathe in, breathe out.
5. Place your right hand over your abdomen while you are breathing. Relax your shoulders, and visualize the internal organs that lie just inside the abdomen that are massaged and supported by the abdominal muscles, the pelvic floor, and the connective tissues that surround them. Feel the nat-

ural rhythm of your breath as it moves your body. Breathe in, breathe out.

6. Place your left hand on your rib cage, and notice how it moves while you are breathing. Visualize the diaphragm that lies just inside your rib cage. This muscle melds with connective tissue and fascia along your thoracic spine. It lies below and is intimately woven into the underside of the cardiac sac that surrounds and protects your heart. Feel the natural rhythm of your breath moving your body. Breathe in, breathe out.

7. Move your right hand from your abdomen, and place it on your upper chest. Notice how it moves while you are breathing. Visualize the lungs and the heart that lie just inside the upper chest. These amazing organs coordinate the exchange of life-bringing oxygen that is extracted from the air, moved through the lung tissue, transported into the blood, and pumped by the heart throughout the entire body. Feel the natural rhythm of your breath moving your body. Breathe in, breathe out.

8. Feel the connection of the front, then the sides, and then the back of your rib cage and torso. Feel the sensation of protection that comes from this amazing bony structure. A structure that allows freedom of movement, maintains protection to the vital organs, and allows motion that massages and invigorates the organs within it. Feel how the natural rhythm of your breath massages and invigorates the organs and influences the gentle mobilization of the thoracic spine while at the same time protecting and vitalizing the internal organs. Breathe in, breathe out.

9. For the next few minutes, allow yourself to rest in this gentle and rhythmic massage. Allow yourself to feel the freedom within the protection. Allow yourself to be present in this breath. To be present in this moment. Allow yourself to—just be.

10. Breathe in, breathe out.

Take a moment every day to stop and bring your attention to your breath. It is your SUPERPOWER!

BREATHING IS OUR SUPERPOWER

Caroline's response to my request to close her mouth and breathe through her nose was one of curiosity. "I've never noticed whether I breathe through my nose or my mouth," she said. I asked her how it felt, as I had not noticed any signs of intolerance. "I am not sure yet. It didn't feel bad. I was just surprised that I'd never noticed how I breathe, that's all."

I smiled with her response and continued with the instruction for diaphragmatic breathing. Caroline followed along with the instructions for hand placement and tolerated lying on her back with her knees bent during the five-minute process. Her face was relaxed, and I could see that she was focusing her attention on every word that I shared in the directions for her practice. Seeing her positive tolerance to the breathing activities allowed me to move forward to begin to advance the practice by asking her to begin to engage the muscles in her abdomen during the exhalation phase of the breath. "Okay, keep breathing smoothly, in and out. On the next breath, I want you to begin to lengthen the exhalation gently."

Caroline nodded in understanding. I could see her focused concentration, trying to keep her attention on her breath and now attempting to add a longer exhalation. I noticed that her breathing lost its smooth rhythm and that her face was getting flushed. "Take rest, Caroline."

She returned to her normal breathing and shared, "I felt like I was doing fine until you asked me for the longer exhale. I just couldn't do it. It felt odd in a way that I can't explain. I felt a bit light-headed in trying."

I told her that her experience is not uncommon. "You were doing something that's unfamiliar to your body right now, and your body was responding well until it began to get tired." I shared, "You are on the right track and at the very beginning stages of your awareness practice. You are now beginning to pay attention to what your body is experiencing, and today, you get a gold star. You noticed a change in your body … that told you, and me—yes, I was watching you—that it was time to take rest. This is a very important lesson from your body. Good work."

Caroline continued to rest on the yoga mat, lying on her back with her knees bent. I guided her to come into sitting on the mat with her legs stretched out ahead of her body on the mat. I continued the instruction and to explain what she could expect in the therapeutic yoga practices that we would be working on in our upcoming sessions together.

"Caroline, the practices that I will be guiding you through over the next few weeks are a thoughtful combination of muscle strengthening and lengthening activities that I have developed to positively influence every major joint in the body, in a very gentle way." I continued to share about how the activities would help her to begin to work on focusing her attention and bring her awareness into the present moment. I reiterated that these basic practices were fundamental building blocks of the Therapeutic Astanga Method© that I developed to help her begin to connect with her body. I shared that focusing her attention on keeping her breath smooth during the physical movements was just one tool among many that she would have at her disposal. Over time and with consistent gentle practice, she would be able to use the breath to help her move away from pain and dysfunction, as she practiced connecting with her body and became more aware of what it needed. This process would help her recognize when she was feeling strong and would also let her know when she was fatiguing and needed to take rest.

"Caroline, the breath will be your guide. Keeping your attention on maintaining smooth and rhythmic breathing when you perform the therapeutic yoga activities is central to success in this practice. How much you do is secondary to how well you are breathing when you do it."

Caroline nodded in understanding and then followed with, "You sure are talking a lot about breathing. I never knew that this therapeutic yoga would focus so much on breathing. I thought that yoga was just about stretching and getting flexible."

I smiled and continued, "You will be participating in a specialized form of breath-centered movement awareness practices that can help you to breathe better and can help start you on the path to a beginning meditation program. I often call it a breath-centered movement meditation."

Caroline shifted on the mat. She had a puzzled expression on her face, as if she was going to ask me a question, but she remained silent.

Help, I've Fallen, and I Can't Get Up

"Okay, we are done for today. You've done great work."

Caroline chimed in, "Oh-oh, it's time to get up off the floor, isn't it?" I nodded, and she continued, "Although the thought of getting back up makes me nervous, I can't stay down here forever. I don't want to be that woman on the TV commercial, 'Help, I've fallen, and I can't get up.'" We both laughed, and I assured her that getting up off the floor was my specialty. Caroline smiled and said, "I'm counting on this."

"Okay now, keep breathing."

I brought Caroline's attention back to the work that we were doing. I wanted to keep her focused and moving because it was time to get up onto her hands and knees to prepare for standing up. "Okay, Caroline, mouth closed, breathe through your nose. Keep breathing softly, and move onto your hands and knees, spread your fingers and thumbs wide. Feel the weight even between the whole surface of both hands. Breathe."

Caroline pressed herself up with purpose, keeping her attention on her breathing.

"I call this the quadruped or four-footed posture. This posture is so important to helping you discover your upper body strength and stability. You did this earlier and will do this again and again in the therapeutic yoga program that will help you get better. It is a basic way to continue to encourage your body to move as it was intended. We are working on encouraging your nervous system to do what she was designed to do. Coming back to the basics."

Caroline said, "I feel like a baby again, learning how to crawl on my hands and knees."

I shared, "There is a connection between the work that I want your nervous system to do in the experience of quadruped posture and the experience of a baby who is learning for the first time. There are many beneficial processes occurring that positively influence your nervous system when you move in and practice this pose."

Getting Up Off the Floor

If you are lying on your back, bend your knees, roll onto your side, and then onto your stomach. Breathe while you are doing this. Come up onto your elbows, and see how that feels. Push into your elbows and knees to lift your hips off the floor, and move onto your hands and knees. Breathe.

Push into the mat/floor using the strength of your arms and hands (with your palms flat and fingers wide). Keep breathing.

Curl your toes under to help your feet move into position to make it easier to lift the knees off the mat. Press up into the downward-facing dog. Breathe.

Widen the stance of your feet as you begin to walk your feet closer to your hands on the mat. Bend your knees, and move your feet towards your hands until your feet are completely in solid contact on the mat. Breathe.

Bring your hands to your thighs. Breathe.

Bring your torso to level with the earth, almost like a tabletop. Hold here and breathe, to help get your blood pressure to level out. Breathe.

Then slowly begin to push through the strength of your legs to straighten your body up back to the standing position. Keep your eyes on a point of reference, a focal point to improve balance. Breathe.

Congratulations, you made it off the floor!

Caroline smiled and said, "Oh, good. I want all the positive benefits that I can get." Then she moved her attention back to breathing gently through her nose with her mouth closed.

I continued, "Okay, now, curl your toes under to get your feet under you, press your hands into the mat, use your strength to lift your knees up off the mat, BREATHE, and lift your butt up into the air. Keep pressing your strong arms into the mat, as if you were trying to push yourself away from the mat. BREATHE! Yes, you are now in the downward-facing dog position. Inhale, exhale, one. Inhale, exhale, two. Keep breathing."

Caroline's breathing began to get a bit louder. I could see her arms begin to tremble.

"Look forward towards your hands, and now step your feet apart to get them wide on your mat. Keep your feet wide apart as you step them to move closer to your hands. Bend your knees as much as you need to, and get your feet flat on the mat as you step them forward. You've got this. Keep breathing."

Caroline's face was beginning to flush, and her breathing was now getting rough.

"Bring your hands to your thighs, lift your torso to a tabletop position, and make sure that your feet are solid on the mat. Stay here for a moment and place your gaze on something in front of you that's not moving to help you keep your balance. BREATHE."

Caroline followed every word, doing her best to keep breathing.

"Now press your strong legs into action to push yourself up away from the floor. Lift your chest and drop your bottom back like you are moving into a deep squat. Keep your spine long. BREATHE! Now use the strength in your legs, and push up to standing. BREATHE."

Caroline followed every command.

"Woooo hoooo! You did it, Caroline!"

Caroline made it back up to the standing position, and beaming, she exclaimed, "I did it. I wasn't sure if I could, but here I am standing." She was perspiring, flushed, and a little out of breath, but smiling. After a moment she said, "Wow, that was hard, but I did it."

"I am so encouraged by the work that you did today, Caroline. You took a challenging situation and made it work for you. Thank you for having the confidence to do this work with me."

Caroline shared, "I am not going to lie, this was hard, and there was a minute where I doubted that I could get up. I am so glad that you were here to help me."

I continued, "This is just part of the process. Now you know what your first homework activities are. In the next few weeks, we will be expanding on the work that you did today. We will work together to make sure that you feel confident in each activity."

A look of concern crossed over Caroline's face when she asked, "There's more?"

I smiled and said, "Yes, there's more work to do, but we're going to go slow with developing your program. There's no rush. It took you a while to get to this point, and it will take a while to get back to your full strength." Caroline let out a sigh of relief, and I continued, "I can see by the work that you were able to do today that you have everything within you to meet your goals of moving independently with less pain. We will be working towards your return to whole mind, body, and spirit balance. Now we need time and some consistent effort on both our parts."

REVIEWING OUR FIRST SESSION AND SETTING UP FOR STEPS AHEAD

We returned to sit in the living room where I shared my thoughts about the results of Caroline's first session. "I know that it might have felt a bit challenging at first, but you did well when moving down onto the floor and getting back up, Caroline." She smiled, and I continued,

We have work to do. Let's start with meeting once per week so that we can develop your therapeutic yoga program. You will have to make time to do your practice every day."

Caroline responded quickly, "I can do that. This is important to me." She paused, "Will I have to get down on the floor?"

I replied, "We will work on getting down on to the floor together, over the next few sessions. One of the goals that I have set for you is to get down to the floor and back up from the floor easily, safely, and independently. You will work on this by practicing the first parts of the Therapeutic Sun Salutation this week. This whole-body activity will warm up your body, set your breathing pattern, and help put your mind in the right space for focusing on your practice. Don't worry about getting all the way down to the floor this week. Just begin with the upper body arm movements and continue to the gentle squat with your hands on your thighs with the spine movements. I want to make sure that you are safe and comfortable with the activity when you are doing it on your own. You can continue to do the rest of your practice lying on the firm surface of your bed for now. We will follow up on your progress next week and get down on the floor together."

I reached into my bag and pulled out a paper copy of the diaphragmatic breathing activities that I wanted her to work on. I also included pages with the rest of her program. I continued, "Diaphragmatic breathing is your next very important homework activity. Three sets of 10 rounds of inhale/exhale, followed by three sets of 10 rounds of breaths with a lengthened exhalation. Keeping your focused attention on maintaining the smooth rhythm of your breathing is more important than how much you do. Shoot for quality in this beginning homework activity."

I shared that the program that we started on that first session was working on setting the foundation for her improved core stability, spine, and major joints mobility. I also gave her a copy of the Therapeutic Sun Salutation represented in pictures on the page.

Did you notice that I mentioned handing my client a paper copy of her therapeutic yoga program? This visit happened in the days before I had access to the digital media that I created for delivering my therapeutic yoga home programs. In fact, it didn't exist like it does now. The internet was in its very early stages. Some of you reading this will remember those days. I did not have a laptop, and high-speed internet (as we know it now) was still 20 years away. To help my clients to remember their programs, I carried a small portable file folder with images and instructions of the most common activities that I would share in a first visit. If I didn't have a copy for a new exercise, I did my best to create the image and write down the instructions on a blank sheet of paper before I left. I could then create an individualized packet for them when I returned to my home office. These days, I take full advantage of the digital world and email my clients links to digital video on my websites or YouTube accounts that I have created over the years. These direct links help my clients follow along and practice with me on video and with my specific instructions for all the activities that we are developing for their home program. This technology has made it easier for my clients to be successful, and I am grateful for having access to it.

We set weekly appointments for the next month. Same time, same day. I encouraged Caroline to do the same thing with her personal home practice to set as close to the same time every day for her homework. Creating a consistent and regular practice is important as it helps to create a habit. Scheduling time for regular exercise and self-care is a good habit to form.

We discussed the approach that I was recommending for our therapeutic yoga program that we were developing together. That we would be taking it one session at a time. I would observe the progress that she had made during the week before our next session, adjust it, and add or subtract activities based on her individual needs. I made sure that Caroline understood that her daily personal practice was mandatory. It was important to help her improve and that it would help me know how she was doing. "The next time I see you, your body will show us if she is tolerating the practice. Be gentle but work with awareness every day. You can call me if you have any questions about your program. I wouldn't be surprised if your body feels some slight soreness tomorrow, but you should not be incapacitated by this work. I will encourage you to repeat these 'slightly offensive activities,' the ones that make your muscles sore. If you keep breathing smoothly while you do the work, your body may soon recognize it as a good thing. Do call me if you have any extreme pain. I want to hear from you although I am not expecting that you will feel more than just a slight reminder of our time together."

Caroline had a look of confidence on her face when we said our goodbyes. I walked out of Caroline's home into the day that was warming up nicely with the sun shining for my drive to my next appointment. I reviewed Caroline's visit in my mind. She had some challenges, but everything about her showed that she was willing to do the work. This made it more likely that she would be successful in improving her state of being, but I could never be certain. I would learn more about this the next time I came to visit.

I added my notes of the day's session to the file that I had started that detailed Caroline's history and the list of goals that we had set for our work together. Caroline's physical, cognitive, and emotional state of being, and the fact that she was not in an active state of pain at the time of our assessment showed that she would not require any other medical or mental supportive care and did not require me to work with her in my capacity as a physical therapist. I would continue to monitor these things during our upcoming sessions, just in case something in her health status changed.

I have to admit that the physical therapist in me never really leaves when I am acting in my capacity as a therapeutic yoga specialist. It is impossible for me to not see my clients any other way, so I don't even try. I just keep my focus on the work at hand, helping clients move closer to their whole mind, body, and spirit health with the gentle, breath-centered awareness practices of the Therapeutic Astanga Method©. I was looking forward to witnessing Caroline's progress in her therapeutic yoga program. I did not get a call from Caroline during the time between our sessions.

CHAPTER **3**

THE SECOND VISIT— HARDER THAN THOUGHT

A week passed and I arrived at Caroline's home for our second session. It was another beautiful day in the outskirts of the Texas Hill Country, the air was crisp and cool, and the sun was shining bright in the clear blue sky. On the drive out to this appointment, I considered what I might find when I arrived. Did Caroline do her prescribed homework? I didn't hear from her after the first session, but did that mean that everything was okay, or did it mean that she was reluctant to contact me? Our first session had gone well, but there are a lot of factors that can get in the way during the week in between sessions. I would get more information about the potential success of the program that we had started during this second visit.

I stepped out of my car into the cool and sunny morning and walked onto her front porch to ring the doorbell. Caroline opened the door, greeted me warmly, and asked, "Will we be starting our work in the fitness room?"

I nodded and replied, "That is a great space to do your work." was encouraged by her enthusiasm.

She was ready for her practice and moving with purpose when she said, "I've been doing my homework, and I have a few questions."

I replied, "This is good to hear. When you have questions, it confirms that you've been doing the work."

Caroline led me to the fitness room where I could see that she had placed a mat, a towel, and a yoga strap on the floor in a neat stack. Caroline removed her shoes and socks and approached her yoga mat. "I have been working on getting closer to the floor. It is harder than I thought."

I shared, "This is true. We are mobilizing every major joint and working some of the largest muscles in your body when we do the Therapeutic Sun Salutation©. It does the job well. That is one of the reasons that I developed it and started to share it with every client that I work with."

Caroline then asked, "I want you to tell me if I am doing this salutation thing right; it feels odd."

I walked towards Caroline to stand next to her and said, "Show me what you have been working on."

Caroline began in standing mountain pose on the first third of her yoga mat and started her practice. She went through the upper body movements, then added the sitting back squat movements, bringing her hands to her thighs. When she began to do the variation of cat/cow in standing, I noticed that her knees would straighten when she extended her spine to look forward. I took a mental note and continued to observe as Caroline widened her stance to squat back while she placed her hands on her thighs. The smooth and rhythmic breathing that Caroline had begun her work with was now beginning to change. It was getting a bit louder, and Caroline's face was beginning to flush. She completed the set of five squats and returned to standing.

"Have a seat on the bench and take rest for a moment, Caroline. Let's review a few things." I gave her feedback about the movement that she was doing at the beginning of the Therapeutic Sun Salutation©. I demonstrated the movement of extension and flexion of the spine in the standing variation of cat/cow and shared about the importance of keeping the knees bent during the execution of this movement. "This activity gives me a lot of information about the restrictions that you might have in your lower body that might influence your spine and other parts of your body that might not seem to be related. When the muscles at the back of your thighs (the hamstrings) are tight, they can pull tension on and influence other parts of your body, like the pelvis and spine. I have asked you to keep your knees bent when you perform this active movement of your spine to reduce the tension of the thigh muscles and possibly help to reduce stress and tension to your low back. Okay, let's try it again." I motioned for Caroline to stand, and we did the work together, this time in slow motion.

Caroline followed along with me as I guided her, "Inhale, extend your spine, exhale, and flex your spine. Inhale, stretch your chest and the frontside of your body as you extend your spine, exhale, and feel the backside of your body stretch while you round through your spine. Keep breathing gently." I noticed that Caroline was moving carefully, as if the movements were unfamiliar. "Pay attention to the sensation of movement in your spine that matches the movement of your breath. Extend your spine on the inhalation, and flex your spine on the exhalation." At the end of five rounds of flexion and extension, I asked Caroline to come back to standing upright.

She said, "I'm not so sure about that movement. It makes me a bit nervous. I can feel the muscles in my back and almost thought that I felt the beginning of a spasm. I'm glad that I didn't get a spasm, but I don't really like that movement." I took a mental note of this and responded, "Caroline, that movement is inviting the muscles in your back to do the work that they were intended to do in your body. You are doing it in standing, and there is a lot that your body must control to make everything happen in a coordinated fashion. I get a lot of information about your readiness for movement when I observe you doing this. Thanks for being patient with me."

Caroline responded, "And my thighs, wow, I could really feel this in the front of my thighs, they were getting tired."

I nodded and shared, "Yes, I noticed that they were beginning to tremble. There will be many activities that I ask you to perform where you will notice your muscles getting tired, and this is not exactly a bad thing. It might not feel comfortable at first, but you will feel it less as you repeat this activity and get stronger. Just make sure that you pay attention to your breath, and stop if you are not breathing smoothly."

Caroline asked, "Are you sure my muscles will get stronger if I keep doing this?"

"Yes. If all goes as planned, your body will realize that you are doing this on purpose, and if everything else in your body is cooperating—for example, if you are well hydrated, have good nutrition, and are getting proper rest—then your body will do everything in its power to help you meet the demands of the activities that you are adding to your life. This could include making more muscle." Caroline smiled as she came back to standing upright. I then shared one of the mantras that supports the Therapeutic Yoga approach that I had developed, "Muscles may get tired, but joints should never hurt." I asked Caroline to remember this as it could help her to avoid doing something that could challenge the safety of her joints and impede the progress in her personal practice.

Caroline shared, "I understand what you are saying, and I will make sure that I keep my knees bent when I move my spine in this sun salutation from now on. I will do the best that I can and hope that it gets a little easier. I have been doing this every day since I saw you last. Now I will do it better." Then she looked over to me with a sly grin on her face and said, "I'm not going to lie. My legs, arms, and body were a little sore the day after your first visit. Even though it was a little uncomfortable, it also kind of felt good, in a weird way. I had not felt muscle soreness from exercise in a long time. I did not have any back spasms, just mild muscle soreness. It went away by the third day. I just kept doing the work that you gave me. I imagine that I might be feeling today's session later this week."

Short Form of the Therapeutic Sun Salutation©

"Okay, now it is time to work on getting down onto the floor. Let's do the short form of the Therapeutic Sun Salutation© since you already started the beginning. Now place your feet wide on the yoga mat, breathe, squat back, and touch the floor with your hands. Straighten your legs, stand up, and then squat back and touch the floor. Keep breathing. Do it again, and this time put your palms flat down on the mat. Keep your fingers and palms wide, keep the weight even between the ball and the heel of both hands, and push the floor away from you and step your feet back into the downward-facing dog. Nice. Hold it for five breaths, then bend the knees to come down onto your hands and knees [quadruped position]."

I continued by guiding Caroline into the practice of the cat/cow posture and followed with the thread the needle posture. I could see that Caroline was getting tired, so I invited her to move into child's pose to rest.

Caroline then said, "Wait a minute, that cat posture felt like what you had me do in standing. This one did not feel as hard. Why is that?"

I explained that her spine had a lot more support in the hands and knees (quadruped) position and that could have made her nervous system trust the motion a little bit more than when she did it in standing. I also shared that her legs did not have to do as much work to keep her upright, and her thigh muscles were in a relaxed position that reduced any tension that they might place on her spine during the movements.

I knew that this was a lot of information to give Caroline at this time. I had already overwhelmed her with our activities and everything else that I was sharing, but she asked me a question, and I always try to answer my clients' questions to the best of my abilities. I also let them know when I don't have an answer. Truthfulness is one of the yoga lifestyles practices that is very important to me. As my clients get to know me, they realize that I have strong opinions about things and that I am not afraid to share those opinions, especially when asked.

After a minute of rest, I guided Caroline through the transition from child's pose, back to quadruped, then back up into downward-facing dog. "Hold for five breaths, Caroline. You can do this." Caroline's arms were shaking, her face was beginning to flush, but she was breathing the best that she could. "Okay, Caroline, step your feet towards your hands, keep the feet wide, bring your hands to your thighs, and set your feet flat on the mat while you bring your torso to a table-top position. Okay, push through those strong legs, and get back to standing. Great job!"

Caroline was flushed but smiling. "I did it again, I made it down to the floor and back up. Every time I do it, it seems a little bit easier."

"This is good to hear, Caroline, because it's time to get back down onto the floor again."

Caroline's brow furrowed for a moment, then her face brightened and she said, "Let's do this."

She was ready, so I guided her back to the floor so that we could review the previous week's practice. Caroline moved carefully, following the instructions that I gave her for her program. She was using her diaphragmatic breathing and took rest when her breath started to get challenged. Overall, she performed well. It was obvious that she had done her homework.

When she rested for a few minutes, I shared with her the importance of learning how to relax and then activate her pelvic floor muscles. "Caroline, the pelvic floor muscles are the foundation of our core muscle stabilizers along with our deep hip flexor and our abdominal and back extensor muscles. They all work together reflexively to help us move through our day and are activated when we lift, push, pull, and move around in our daily living. Our culture has been a bit shy about talking about the perineal area and the pelvic floor muscles. I like to make sure that you are aware of these important muscles and how when these muscles have a healthy balance of elasticity and strength, they engage reflexively to help support you in your daily living. They also play an integral role in support of our pelvic and internal organs."

"Are you talking about doing Kegels? I can never remember to do those. Do I have to do those too?" Caroline looked intent.

I replied, "I am referring to the muscles that are being activated when we do a Kegel, the pelvic floor muscles. They are the foundation of your core and lie in the lowest part of your pelvis, connected to your tailbone and your pubic bone at the underside and front of your pelvis. Here's some good news. You have already started working on them just by practicing your breathing activities. When you lengthen your exhalation, they get the opportunity to shorten and move closer to the center of your body. When you inhale gently, these muscles expand out and away from your center as they respond to the changes in your abdomen when the diaphragm moves down away from the chest area. It's a reflex and the movements are very efficient. This is just one more reason to do your breathing practices regularly, they are good for you on so many levels. For now, we will keep things simple and let your breathing activities do the work. You won't have to do anything special with these muscles."

Caroline smiled, "I like knowing that my breathing activities are helping these muscles work to become more relaxed and stronger at the same time. I never thought that they needed to be flexible too. The human body is truly amazing."

"I agree, Caroline, we are a most incredible creation, every part of us in place for a specific purpose. Okay, it's time for you to get back up off the mat."

Caroline responded, "I'm ready," as she proceeded to roll onto her side, transition to her hands and knees, and press up into downward-facing dog. She stayed in downward-facing dog for three breaths and then began to walk her feet to her hands and paused before she stood up. She was flushed but was able to keep her breathing fairly under control. "I believe that I am getting the hang of this, it is feeling easier every time I do it."

I responded, "Thank you for doing the work, Caroline. You are on your way to being stronger and more mobile every day."

We reviewed the activities for that session, and I asked her to continue the breathing activities and the beginning of the Therapeutic Sun Salutation© as her daily homework. Caroline asked good questions that let me know that she was really paying attention and interested in making the changes necessary and doing the work to meet her goals.

"I will see you next week, and we will continue the adventure."

Caroline walked with me to her front door, and we said our good-byes. I walked into the cool sunshine of the late morning to my car, where I made a few notes for my records and left Caroline's neighborhood to go to my next scheduled appointment.

Caroline was showing commitment to her practice and was invested in making an improvement in her well-being. The following weeks would get easier because we would be repeating the practices that form the foundation of her therapeutic yoga program and at the same time, these next few weeks could become more challenging because she would be repeating the same practice daily. The newness would begin to fade, and it would test Caroline's commitment to the program.

CHAPTER 4

WEEK THREE: A CONCERN

I received an email from Caroline during the week between sessions. She wanted to remind me that she had a few questions that
she wanted to ask me about the practices that we had started. I
made notes in her file and noted this request in my schedule.

When I arrived at Caroline's home for our third session, the wind was
beginning to blow, and a mild cold front had moved through the Hill
Country bringing with it much needed rain and cooler temperatures.
I walked up to the front steps, and Caroline opened the door before
I could reach for the bell.

"Good morning. It looks like you're ready for our session."

Caroline invited me into her home and said, "Can we sit down for a
moment before we go into the fitness room? I have something that
I want to ask you about."

I responded with a nod, saying, "Yes, of course. I had a note on my
calendar to remind you about this. What did you want to ask?" We
sat down on separate cushioned chairs in her front living area.

Caroline looked past me and out of the front window, and I noticed
that she was avoiding eye contact. This concerned me since this was
unlike the usual manner that she interacted with me on our previous
visits. "Caroline, what did you want to ask me?"

She shifted in her chair and then turned to meet my gaze and began. "I have been thinking about something that you mentioned
in our first session." She paused and looked down to her hands.
Her expression changed, and a look of concern came over her face
as she said, "You mentioned that we were doing meditation." She
shifted her body uneasily in her chair again and then quietly said,
"I was wondering," she paused, "I don't mean any disrespect, but

what did you mean about our doing meditation in the practice? Is there something that I need to know about my program? I know that we are doing yoga, but I didn't think that we were going to meditate. Is there something more about these practices that I should be aware of?"

She continued, "I mentioned to one of my friends that I had a few visits with a physical therapist and that we were using yoga to help with my back. She told me to be careful with doing yoga and to especially make sure to avoid meditation."

The look of concern in Caroline's eyes and the sound of her voice let me know that this was an important time in the session for me to continue to listen with an open mind and a compassionate heart.

Caroline continued, "My friend said that her pastor told the whole congregation that yoga and meditation were methods that allowed 'evil' into a Christian's heart."

I took a gentle breath in and out and continued to listen as she continued, "Will I have to become a Buddhist or pray to some foreign gods to practice yoga? I really enjoyed the breathing and the movement practices that we were doing. Is this yoga and meditation practice going to affect my faith or make me change my religion?"

I responded, "Thank you, Caroline, for asking this important question and letting me know about your concerns." I continued by sharing that yoga and meditation were not a religion and that to the best of my knowledge, I understood that yoga and meditation practices have been included in many religious practices over many years. I gave the example of prayer that was used in many religions and practiced in many unique ways. I shared that prayer could be considered a form of meditation because in praying we are focusing our attention on something, like having a conversation with God. I continued that many of us might find comfort in the practice of prayer, especially when we are in a difficult place or need spiritual support.

I shared with Caroline that I was a woman of faith and that before I had begun my studies and personal practice, I too was concerned about the question of yoga being a religion. I wanted to understand and see for myself, so I decided to do research and study to learn as much as I could about the ancient practices. In my continued study of the ancient writings about the yoga lifestyle, I learned that, indeed, yoga was not a religion but was a lifestyle practice that has been used by some to enhance religious practices and that it was experienced by many individuals, especially in India where it originated.

I added, "Practicing therapeutic yoga has not changed my religion, but it has made a positive impression on my own faith in my creator and in my own self. Before I began to study and practice yoga mindfulness and meditative techniques, I had never thought much about the way that I prayed. I used to have this one-sided conversation with God. Me asking for things and making promises, me always talking and talking to God. I never realized that my prayer time pretty much reflected my daily living habits. Me always talking, asking questions, demanding answers, and never stopping to settle and to get quiet. I would not stop talking long enough to listen. To hear God speak. My personal yoga practice helped me to begin the process of quieting the constant conversations in my mind. It helped me to feel more comfortable in the stillness, in the quiet spaces. This has helped me immensely over the years."

Caroline was looking at me now with a compassionate expression when she said, "I completely understand what you're saying although I have never thought about mindfulness and prayer like this before."

There was a stillness in the room that made the sound of the wind outside seem louder. Caroline was in deep thought. The stillness broke when I said, "Well, now that we've unlocked some of the secrets of the universe, what do you think about this yoga and mindfulness stuff? Do we need to stop? I'm not here to force you to participate in anything that you aren't comfortable with. You won't hurt my feelings, and I will understand completely if you have had a change of heart about participating in therapeutic yoga with me."

Caroline looked at me with a twinkle in her eyes and said in a hushed tone, "You know, that friend that I told you about? Well, I never had much faith in many of the things that she has shared with me over the years. I'm not worried about this yoga thing being evil. I want to continue and see how it works for me. So far, everything that we've been doing has made me feel better."

"If you're interested, I would be happy to share some of the books that I have about the history and philosophy of the yoga lifestyle so that you can do your own research."

Caroline and I got up and walked back to the fitness room to continue our session. While we walked, she said, "I'd like to read about yoga and appreciate your offering to share some of your books. I love to learn."

Caroline stepped onto her mat, and we started the Therapeutic Sun Salutation. She moved down onto the mat and continued to focus her attention on maintaining smooth, gentle, and rhythmic breathing, as we reviewed the activities that she performed during our last session.

I am grateful for this work that allows me the opportunity to support the improving function of individuals with varied histories of physical and functional limitations. The one-on-one sessions allow me the opportunity to connect with my clients on a regular basis to support them in their return to activities that they might have been familiar with before a setback or to explore activities that may be new to them. The practices that I develop with my clients are based on focusing attention on the breath to help improve concentration and to bring their attention to the present moment. This creates a mindful breath-centered movement awareness practice that can be considered a form of meditation. I feel that it is important to share this with my clients early in the work. I am always interested to hear what they think about meditation.

THE POWER OF THE NERVOUS SYSTEM TO BRING THE BODY INTO BALANCE

Caroline moved with awareness from child's pose, onto her hands and knees (quadruped pose), and then she moved down onto the mat to lie on her back with her knees bent for a brief rest period. It was the perfect opportunity for a teaching moment.

"I want to tell you why it is important to keep our attention on maintaining smooth and rhythmic breathing during our practice and daily living activities."

Caroline listened intently while I explained. "There are situations where our nervous system, which is the command center of the whole body, gets overwhelmed. There are many reasons for this to occur and often related to times when a person is struggling with an injury, illness, a surgery, or a stressful life event. When this happens, the nervous system can automatically shift into a state of emergency that activates the stress response, technically known as the sympathetic nervous system response, to try to help us through the difficult situation. Adrenaline and other hormones are circulated within the body system to help it prepare to 'fight for life.' This automatic process can be a real lifesaver in an emergency."

Caroline adjusted her position on the yoga mat and said, "You're talking about fight or flight. I've heard about this."

I continued, "If the nervous system stays in a state of hypervigilance, where the stress response is continuously active, it can begin to take a toll on the smooth functioning of all the body systems and organs that are working to keep us in a state of balanced health. The body that responded so well to the sudden influx of the stress hormones that helped it to fight for life or move it out of danger is now challenged by these hormones that are constantly circulating in the bloodstream. This can cause changes to the normal function of our primary internal organ systems when the levels of stress hormones remain elevated over the long term since the hormonal influx is designed primarily to help us in short-term emergencies."

Caroline sighed, "This sounds very familiar, I can remember times when I was beginning my work as a realtor and my kids were in middle school. I was working 70-plus hours a week, only to return home to continue working on the tasks that were important to meet the needs of my family and friends. Trying to keep it all together and make it look like everything was okay. I didn't sleep very much during those days."

"I understand how this can happen, Caroline. I'm working part-time around my family, and I just love this work, but all my responsibilities to my home and family are waiting for me when I get back. It can get difficult at times, but we do have tools to help us. The opposite of the stress response is often referred to as the relaxation response, technically known as the parasympathetic nervous system response. Among its many responsibilities, the parasympathetic nervous system monitors and allows the important processes that regulate the optimal functioning of our internal organs and their normal functions like digestion, elimination, breathing, circulation of important hormones, the regenerative process of healing, the immune response, etc. This process is often referred to as the relaxation response."

Caroline's eyes brightened when she exclaimed, "I love the sound of that."

I continued, "When the parasympathetic nervous system is engaged and dominant, the circulatory and nervous system activity is diverted from the muscles and organ systems that had been on high alert in fight-or-flight mode. During this shift, activity is directed towards the internal organs working to renew, regenerate, and repair the body to bring it back to a balanced state of optimum functioning. This regenerative process can often cause us to feel lethargic, sleepy, rested, calm, and relaxed. When the nervous system, the internal organs, and body systems are functioning efficiently, the healing process just happens, the body moves back into balance, and we get back to our previous level of physical, mental, and emotional functioning. In some situations, not entirely understood by science, the body gets sidetracked when the nervous system is overwhelmed, over stressed, and often in these situations, healing is delayed, and the body stays in a state of imbalance. This can promote conditions in the body systems that can cause suffering in the form of chronic conditions, pain, and illness."

To reiterate—there are so many reasons for a person to experience pain that are not always directly connected to physical injury. Many of these things can be traced back to experiences of traumatic events, grief, anxiety, depression, isolation, the list is ongoing. Sometimes the client only begins to become aware of this connection when they begin the grounding and connecting-to-self processes that they experience in therapeutic yoga. The nature of the pain experience is different for each person, and that is one of the reasons that I share these therapeutic yoga methods with my clients and am now sharing them with you, the reader.

Even though it is not always easy for my clients when they make this connection, I am always encouraged by the progress that they are making that can then prepare them for consulting with other specialists who can continue to support their progress more effectively, thus bringing the client closer to resolving their personal experiences and possibly moving away from pain for a lifetime.

My goal is to empower the individual with a practice of therapeutic yoga that can be a starting point of a process that can help them to begin to walk on the path to wholeness.

"It sounds like my body is doing a lot of work behind the scenes to try to keep me healthy."

"Yes, Caroline, the rhythmic breathing that I have asked you to bring your attention to is the most important part of your therapeutic yoga practice because it helps to activate the parasympathetic nervous system to help calm your body and encourage restoration. When we focus on lengthening the exhalation, this stimulates the parasympathetic nervous system even more and helps to move us out of the fight-or-flight system. These responses exist in our body systems to help balance them out in our day-to-day living."

Caroline's face brightened, "Now I understand why you want me to keep breathing in my therapeutic yoga practice. It makes sense that I should do this; I want to help my body as much as I can. So far, I have enjoyed the breathing focus and the activities. There may just be hope for me after all."

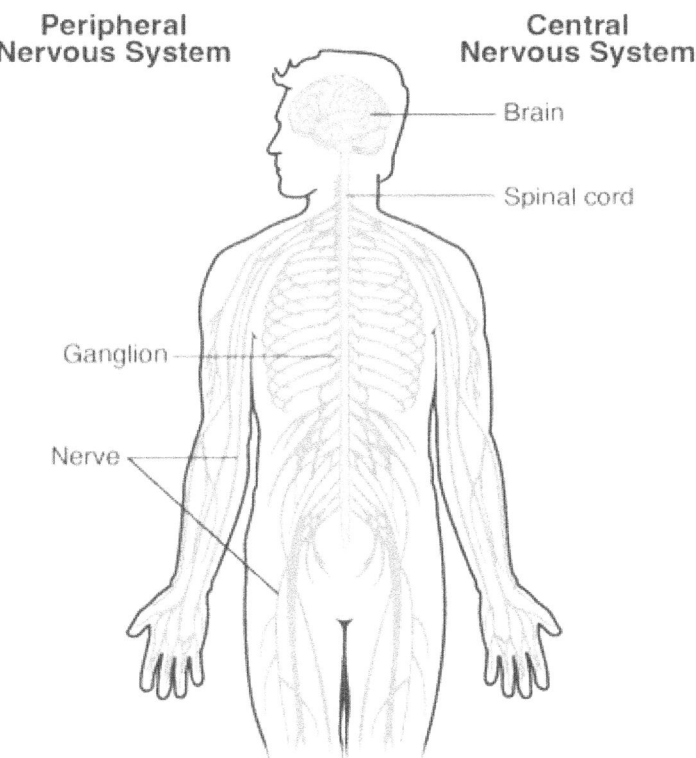

Basic Nervous System

- Central Nervous System: Brain and spinal cord
- Peripheral Nervous System: Peripheral nerves that help brain communicate with the body, receive information, and send signals that cause action
- Autonomic Nervous System: The internal communication system for our internal organs and systems that automatically occur without our having to consciously make them happen.

AUTONOMIC NERVOUS SYSTEM

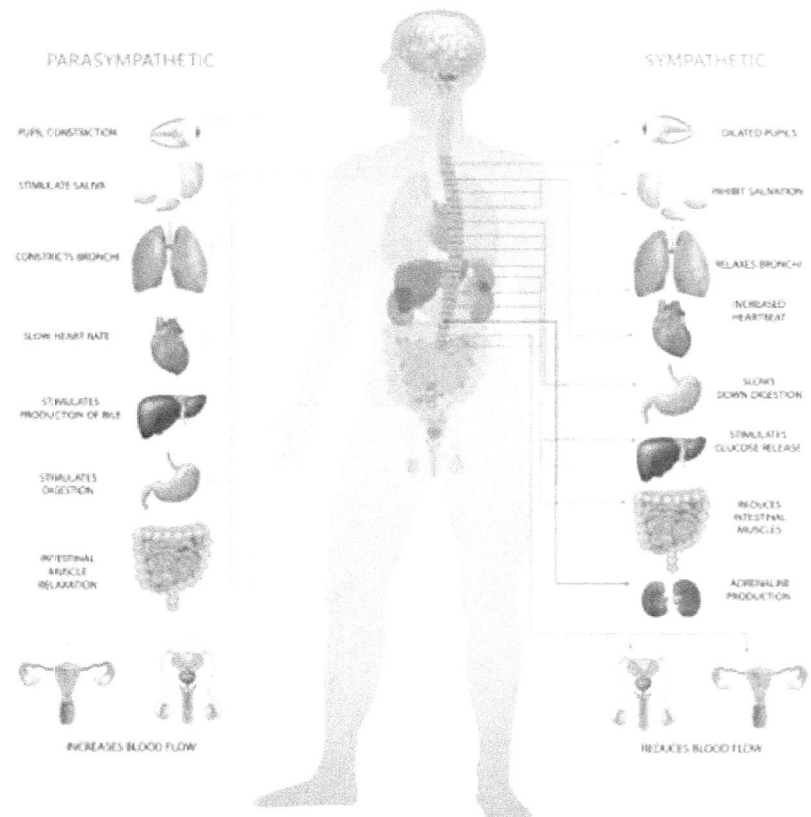

Nervous System: A Basic Review

The nervous system is the command center for the entire body. It is made up of an intricate network of nerves and other structures that communicate information throughout and support the optimum functioning of the body.

The nervous system is made up of two parts: the central nervous system and the peripheral nervous system.

The central nervous system is made up of the brain and spinal cord that lies within the bony spinal column. The brain uses nerves to send messages to different parts of the body.

The peripheral nervous system is made up of the nerves that extend from the central nervous system, exit from the bony spinal column, and branch out to the organs, arms, legs, fingers, and toes.

The peripheral nervous system contains the somatic (body) nervous system, which controls voluntary movements of the body, and the autonomic nervous system, which directs the automatic activities that we don't have to think about, the activities in our body that we don't have to control.

The autonomic nervous system is organized and directed by the tenth cranial nerve, the vagus nerve. Two branches make up the autonomic nervous system and are typically identified as the sympathetic nervous system and the parasympathetic nervous system.

Fight-or-Flight versus Rest-and-Digest

The fight-or-flight response is a whole-body reaction that is caused by the sympathetic nervous system. This causes coordinated changes in organ and tissue function that increases delivery of oxygen and nutrient-rich blood to the working muscles in our body. The heart rate and ability of the heart muscle to contract are increased, so that the heart can pump more blood per minute. The sympathetic nervous system influences a constriction of the blood vessels that feed the organs of the gastrointestinal system and the kidneys to redirect blood towards the muscles that need it to help us fight or run for our lives. The lungs are influenced in that they experience an improved movement of air that maximizes their ability to take in oxygen and eliminate carbon dioxide from the body. The liver's ability to break down glycogen into glucose and form new glucose from noncarbohydrate sources within helps to increase the concentration of glucose (blood sugar) molecules in the blood. This is important because glucose is the source of energy for the brain to be able to accomplish its necessary tasks. There is also a breakdown of fat tissue in the body that increases the fatty acid molecules in the blood, which helps the skeletal muscles contract. Sweating helps the body regulate its temperature during the increased physical activity. The eyes adjust, pupils dilate, so the lens can receive light and adjust to improve distance vision.

The parasympathetic nervous system, often referred to as the "rest-and-digest" response, decreases the heart rate, which helps to conserve energy during resting conditions. Saliva production increases to help with swallowing, and stomach activity is stimulated to help in the processing of food. The intestines are stimulated to continue processing food and absorbing nutrients. The pancreas is stimulated to secrete hormones that help to break down food in the intestine, and this includes insulin that is released to promote the storage of nutrients once they are absorbed by the body. The urinary bladder is also stimulated in this system, which results in urination. The eyes adjust for near vision. This system allows for all the important functions of the internal organs to occur that help us to optimize our health. These things are happening automatically and outside of our control, so it is easy to forget just how important this system is.

"I'm glad that you feel that way, Caroline. And there is more to this breathing that is happening behind the scenes. While the brain is the coordinating center of the nervous system that keeps the intricate network of our whole-body systems in balance and functioning properly, it relies on having adequate levels of oxygen to function effectively. Food that breaks down into blood sugar (glucose) and water, among many other things, is also important to the brain, but not nearly as important as oxygen. Glucose [blood sugar] is also important, and so is water, but these are not nearly as important as oxygen. We can survive for a few weeks without food and a few days without water, but we can only survive a few minutes without oxygen before the important cells of the brain begin to perish and severe damage or death follows. That is what makes breathing such a gift. It is our SUPERPOWER! When we breathe smoothly, rhythmically, and gently, our lungs are capable of transporting oxygen effectively, delivering it efficiently into the bloodstream. The brain and nervous system can sense that everything is okay, all our normal bodily processes can continue, and we never even have to think about it.

"But when we hold our breath, when the breath is challenged or difficult, there's a microscopic dip in the amount of oxygen that is delivered to the brain. This dip is not life-threatening, but the brain really enjoys having ample supply of oxygen, so when the levels dip, even just a little bit, the brain goes into overdrive to try to get more oxygen. Muscles in the entire body get tense and ready to fight for oxygen. Energy gets diverted from the internal organ systems like the gut and other internal organs that are working for us in the background, kidneys, pancreas, etc. All the energy goes towards getting the body ready to fight for oxygen. If a person is already experiencing joint or muscle pain, it could make them feel more pain. Not fun. When a body is breathing efficiently, getting ample oxygen, the nervous system remains calm, the muscles in the body can relax, the organ systems can continue to do what they do without interruption. This can allow the healing, and regenerative processes to occur and/or continue."

Caroline responded, "I didn't know that my nervous system did that. I guess I've never thought much about how my body systems work." She shifted her body while she was lying on her back.

"Do you need to change positions?" I asked.

She responded, "Yes, please, let me roll onto my side for a moment."

I asked if I could go to the living room to get some throw pillows from her couch. She said yes, so I moved into the next room and returned quickly with two fluffy pillows. "Here, let's place this cushion under your head and the other between your knees to help support and level your thighs and pelvis. How does that feel?"

I took this opportunity to share about how using proper support under the head and between the legs when in the side-lying position can reduce tension to the spine and hips.

Caroline noted, "Hey, that does feel good. I'll try that when I go to bed tonight. Although I'm not sure what my husband is going to say about my new pillow friends. He already kids me about the cutrageous mountain of decorative pillows that are on our bed and the nighttime ritual of taking them off before we go to bed every night. This will be fun to watch." I nodded in understanding as we both laughed at the imagined scenario.

After a minute, I removed the pillows and asked Caroline to return to her position lying on her back. "How are you feeling now?" I asked.

With a slight flush to her cheeks she responded, "I'm tired. I had no idea that breathing with awareness and learning about how the body and mind work could take so much out of me."

I took the opportunity to let Caroline rest as I explained, "The practices that we're working on might seem basic and not be very impressive to the outside observer, but they are very powerful. They are working the body systems on a cellular and energetic level. We need to pay close attention to our hydration, nutrition, and mental, emotional, and stress levels, and make sure that we get optimum sleep when we are participating in mind, body, and spirit practices like the ones that we're using in this program. Honoring our body and preparing it for our practice will encourage it to heal and return to balance more effectively after a session. Breathe gently. Let your nervous system know that it has everything that it needs right now."

After a few gentle breaths, I noticed Caroline's face return to normal, no more flushed cheeks. It was time to continue.

STABILITY IN QUESTION

"Okay, Caroline, we have a bit more work to do before we're done today." She was lying on her back when I instructed, "Keep breathing, and reach your arms forward to your thighs. Breathe. Now lift your head off the mat and let your chin come to your chest. Breathe. See if you can hold this position for three breaths. Inhale and exhale, one. Inhale and exhale, two. Inhale and exhale, three."

I could see that Caroline was struggling with this activity, so I quickly placed the index and middle finger of my right hand on her abdomen, a few inches above her belly button and immediately felt the dip in the center of her abdomen that I had begun to suspect might be there. She was shaky in the activity and holding her breath. I encouraged her to breathe and then to release back down to lying on the mat. "Take rest." I got the information that I needed and added this to my mental notes.

Caroline shared, "I haven't done abdominal crunches in a very long time. I used to like doing them when I was in an exercise class with friends quite a few years ago. This was before my kids were born. Once the kids came, it seems like I had less time for myself. I was working part-time around my family and taking the kids to all their activities. I didn't realize that I could lose this strength. I felt so shaky. I did not like that feeling."

I nodded in understanding. We had experienced similar paths although she was 30 years ahead of me at that time. We were women who had started our professional careers, gotten married, and then taken a few detours around our professional path to incorporate starting a family, working on and not always succeeding in balancing our personal, professional, and family lives. I made a mental note to myself, "Don't ever stop. Keep doing what you are doing to try to keep your personal fitness routine."

I congratulated her on her success at surviving the challenges of raising a family and the accomplishments that she had made in her professional life. "We have to help you get your personal fitness and health back on top of the priority list." And with that, I asked her to come back into her smooth and rhythmic breathing activity and proceeded to introduce her to the therapeutic bridge position one. It goes something like this. If you are listening to this right now, take a moment to lie down on a mat or supported surface. If you are reading this, you might want to refer to my website at TherapeuticYogaWorks.com.

Therapeutic Bridge Position One

Lie on your back with your knees bent. Eyes open, look towards the ceiling. Close your mouth and bring your attention to the feeling of the breath moving gently in and out of your nose. Bring your awareness to your feet that are positioned hip distance apart. Lift your toes, and sense the weight of your feet falling even between the ball of the foot and the heel, even between the right and the left foot. Breathe in, breathe out.

Keep your knees upright and vertical, and bring your attention to your hips as they contact the mat. Feel the weight of your hips settle evenly on the mat, right to left side. Breathe in, breathe out.

Notice the space along your low back. There may be a lot of space or very little space. The amount is not important now, but rather how comfortable your low back feels. If it feels good, keep your low back exactly where it is. Breathe in, breathe out.

If your low back feels tension, keep breathing while you shift your low back to gently begin to move it slightly towards the mat, or gently move it slightly away from the mat. Find the most comfortable place for your low back. Once there, hold that position. Breathe in, breathe out.

Now bring your attention to the rib cage and then the shoulder blades that are contacting the mat on the backside of your body. Notice how these parts of your body are settling into the mat. Make any adjustments necessary to bring these areas as close to balance along the right and the left sides of your back body. Breathe in, breathe out.

Draw the shoulder blades towards the center of your back, as if you were trying to hold a winning lotto ticket between them. While you do this, keep your attention on your arms as they rest along the side of your body. Breathe in, breathe out.

Walk the fingers down towards your feet to feel a stretch at your neck and shoulders. Stretch the fingers wide, and set the open palms and wide fingers onto the mat alongside your hips. Breathe in, breathe out.

Bring your attention to the place between your shoulder blades. Did it arch off the mat? If it did, keep breathing while you gently encourage the upper middle back between your shoulder blades to move down towards the mat. It might not go completely flat; it doesn't have to. Just bring your awareness to the subtle muscle activation that begins in this area between your shoulder blades and how it influences the front of your torso and abdominals. Breathe in, breathe out.

Bring your attention to your neck, and begin to lengthen energetically from the top of your head, along the length of your spine, down to the tip of your tailbone. Lengthen your neck as you draw your shoulders down and away from both ears. Keep your gaze on the ceiling; gently press the back of your head into the mat. Breathe in, breathe out. This should feel good. Like you are being energetically lengthened along the mat.

Keep breathing as you begin to press your arms into the mat with the weight balanced evenly between the ball of the hand and the heel of the hand. Stretch your fingers wide. Feel the work, an energetic muscular activation that begins at the back of the shoulders and extends down the arms, crossing the elbow, forearm, and then into the strength of your hands that are evenly positioned on the mat. Breathe in, breathe out.

Keep this upper body activation happening as you breathe smoothly and gently throughout the effort. Bring your attention back to your feet and their position on the mat. Your thighs as they are positioned with knees bent. Begin to press the feet into the mat. Firm the muscles on your hands, arms, thighs, and engage your buttocks. Breathe in, breathe out.

Keep the breath smooth and rhythmic while you engage the entire backside of your body, to strengthen the backside and lengthen the frontside of your body. To begin to bring balance to the body. Breathe in, breathe out.

When it feels comfortable, keep all the action in your muscles and begin to lift the hips evenly from the mat. Pressing the flat palms and the supported feet into the mat. Working the arms and legs, engage the buttocks to lift the hips as high as you can. Keep your breath rhythmic and steady. Breathe in, breathe out.

Hold this position for five breaths. Inhale, exhale—one. Inhale, exhale—two. Inhale, exhale—three. Inhale, exhale—four. Inhale, exhale—five. Keep the firm connection of your arms and smooth breath while you slowly lower your hips back to the mat. Then release all muscular effort. Take rest. Breathe in, breathe out.

Caroline was following along as I guided her through the therapeutic bridge position one. She kept her gaze on the ceiling and focused attention on her breath. Everything was going well until I asked her to press her arms into the mat. I noticed that there was a slight pause in her breath. "Breathe while you press," I said. She regained her rhythm with this reminder.

She moved through the sequence, working the muscles along the backside of her body, lengthening the frontside of her body, trying to lift her hips. Caroline's legs started to shake as she attempted the lift. She held her breath and then said in a panic, "I'm getting a cramp in the back of my left leg."

I responded, "Keep breathing, Caroline. Let go of the effort in your arms, relax your body, straighten your leg out, make a muscle at the front of your thigh, and push your heel away from your center; that will help the cramp go away."

She did as I asked and responded, "Hey, that works. I need to do that when I get a cramp in the middle of the night."

She moved her legs back into the bent knee position while she was lying on her back. I asked her to rest for a moment and then guided her, "Bring your attention back to keeping smooth and gentle breathing."

After a minute of rest, I asked her if she was ready to continue. She responded affirmatively, so I asked her to stretch out on the mat first her right leg and then her left leg while she was lying down on her back.

"OUCH! That really bothers my low back when both of my legs are out straight like that."

I asked her to keep breathing smoothly and to return to lying with her knees bent. I made a mental note, "Check her deep hip flexors for tightness that might be a source of pain."

"Let's keep moving; breathe in, breathe out," I said, guiding her into the next movement.

At this point, it might seem like I was torturing her, but I wanted to get more information and possibly uncover the source or at least partial source of her pain.

WHAT'S CORE GOT TO DO WITH IT?

I asked her to keep breathing, "Now invite your right knee in towards your chest, and hold on to it with your arms. If that feels okay, bring your left knee in too."

She sighed and said, "Oh, this feels so much better than that last movement. It feels good to feel the stretch along my low back like this." She stayed in this supine knees-to-chest stretch position for a few minutes.

"Breathe in, breathe out. Soft, smooth, and gentle." I guided her to keep her breath rhythmic and steady. When she settled into her breath, I asked her to put one foot down and then the other on the mat, returning to lying on her back with her knees bent.

I reached for one of the pillows and placed it under Caroline's legs, behind her knees to help support her lower body and put her low back at ease. "Close your eyes and take rest for a minute. Let your whole body drop into the mat. Bring your attention to the sensation of your breath as it moves your abdomen, the front of your ribs and chest, and the sides and back of your ribs. Allow your arms and legs to release any tension that you might be holding. Allow your neck and shoulders to drop into the mat. Feel your spine and pelvis settle into the mat. For the next few minutes, just settle into the support of the mat and the rhythm of your breath. This is savasana, a purposeful time to take rest." I sat on the floor next to Caroline in silent support of her resting practice.

It is important to take rest at the end of your practice—savasana

The time spent in the supported resting position can help to release any residual muscular tension that the body might be holding after the active physical practices. The resting supportive practice can help to calm the nervous system and return the breath to the normal resting state. When we take rest at the end of our therapeutic yoga practice, we allow the body to integrate all the components of the practice that we have just experienced. This allows the body, mind, and metabolic system to assimilate the breath-centered strengthening, lengthening, and mobilizing awareness practice that you experienced. I like to encourage my clients to focus their attention on observing the natural rhythm of their breath during the resting practice. This continued mindfulness practice can allow the nervous system to drop more deeply into the parasympathetic (regenerative) state and potentially encourage more effective relaxation.

The time spent in the supported lying-down position (which can also be modified to meet the needs of the individual) is as important as the time spent in the active therapeutic yoga practice. This is where the magic happens.

At the end of the five-minute rest time, I guided Caroline to keep breathing while she moved gently back to the seated position, then to her hands and knees, back to the downward-facing dog, then back to standing upright. I noticed that she moved with awareness, keeping her attention on maintaining smooth breathing. Her practice was making an impact already. This was a good sign.

I asked Caroline to take a seat on a bench in the fitness studio so that we could review the day's work and the addition to her home program, which included the therapeutic bridge posture that she would perform three times and hold each for five breaths, followed by the supine knees-to-chest posture, and then the supine lying posture with pillow for support at the back of her knees. I asked her to stay in each posture for five breaths or longer as she felt comfortable.

I then continued with a brief introduction to the importance of beginning an outdoor (when possible) walking program in her neighborhood. Caroline was to begin with walking for five minutes in one direction out of her home and then return so that she could total a 10-minute walk. I asked her to do this at least three times per week. Eventually, we would increase that to a daily walking program.

Caroline asked if she could use her husband's treadmill for indoor walking on cold or wet days. This led to a review of proper use of treadmill for safety. We took the next five minutes getting Caroline comfortable with the treadmill since she had not used this appliance before but had previous experience with some in her past. She demonstrated good balance and coordination and use of the treadmill and its safety features, so we added, either outdoor or slow indoor walking on the treadmill, holding on to the safety rails for improved balance.

We ended our session, and Caroline walked with me to her front door when she shared, "Thank you for answering my questions about meditation and helping me learn how to work the treadmill. I can't believe that I never once thought about using it. To be honest, I've spent more time in the fitness room in the last month than I have since we built this home. I even think that I'm in here more often than my husband is. He's got some catching up to do." We both laughed heartily as we walked through the house to her front door. Caroline's expression got serious again when she turned to me and said, "I'm so happy to have started this program. I know that it is going to make a big difference in my life. I really appreciate our time together."

I responded with a smile, "I really enjoy this work, and I am grateful that you allowed me to be on your whole-health team. You really are progressing nicely."

With that I turned to the door, we said our goodbyes, and I walked out to face the cooler temperature of the day, pleased with the progress of that day's work with Caroline. I was encouraged by her ability to share her questions and concerns about meditation. It is important to me that my clients know as much about how to care for their body as they want to know and to understand the foundation of the practices that I have been melding together to create the Therapeutic Astanga Method© that influences the work that I share with them. My desire to help my clients and "do no harm" extends beyond just their physical health, but also includes their mental, emotional, and spiritual health.

Walking for Exercise Improves Muscular Endurance

I always recommend that my clients who are experiencing back pain participate in a program that also includes some form of cardiovascular activity. The most common that I recommend is walking for exercise. There are so many benefits that a person can access when they begin and continue a regular walking program—improvements in mental health and improvements in muscular endurance that carries over to performance with other exercise programs and functional living requirements.

Muscular endurance can be associated with strength conditioning and cardiovascular conditioning activities like cycling, swimming, running, dancing, walking, and other movement processes that involve having the body sustain movement over time. When it is attributed to walking for exercise, it can be considered the ability of a group of muscles that are able to perform repetitive contractions against a force for an extended period. You might consider that the higher the muscular endurance, then possibly you may be better able to perform the walking activity for a greater period.

Merriam-Webster defines "endurance" as "the ability to withstand hardship or adversity, especially the ability to sustain a prolonged stressful effort or activity."

Over the years that I have worked with persons who were experiencing back pain, I noticed a relationship between the degree of pain that they are living with and their overall endurance.

Those with the most pain tend to have less muscular endurance and are not as active. Those who are active, tend to have less back pain. I have always found it interesting and have wondered which came first. Was it the gradual reduction of physical activity combined with posture challenges and/or injury that caused an increase in the perception of pain and then subsequently a reduction in muscular endurance? Or did the onset of pain due to postural challenges or injury cause the person to be less mobile and then cause a reduction in overall muscular endurance?

There is solid evidence that suggests that lumbar stabilizing exercises coupled with walking for exercise relieves back pain and prevents chronic low back pain by improving overall muscular endurance. I have witnessed a reflection of these types of findings in working with my clients over the years. Those who had the most pain also tended to have less endurance. They were less physically active, and that lack of movement influenced many other parts of their daily functioning.

Research has also shown that participating in regular exercise like stabilization and endurance/walking activities can help to reduce pain perception. I have also seen this in my clients over the years. I have personally experienced this and have witnessed the benefits that come from setting a solid foundation in therapeutic yoga practices and how it carries over to helping a person manage their daily functional living tasks.

A Note About Savasana, The Resting Posture

I get a lot of information about the state of being that my clients are in when I guide them into the resting phase of their therapeutic yoga practice. Some of my clients are fatigued at the end and are ready to take rest. They drop into the supine position with a blanket behind their knees very easily. I can hear their rhythmic breath *cycles, and it tells me that they are responding well to the position. I have had quite a few clients begin to drop off into a light sleep. It is obvious when they are dropping into sleep because their breathing pattern relaxes, and, in some cases, it is true, a few have begun to snore. I try to assure my clients that this is not unusual. I might share that snoring can happen for a variety of reasons, many due to the position of the head and neck when lying down, just in case they feel awkward or embarrassed by this. And then there are a few clients that I have worked with for many years that drop into a very deep resting state, some who might be reading this book right now. You know who you are. It is always an adventure bringing them gently back to the waken state to help them get back into their day.*

Can't Lie Still for Long

Over the years of guiding persons in therapeutic yoga practices, I have met individuals who struggle in the relaxation portion at the end of the practice. I can see it in the way that they keep a foot or hand moving while they lie on the mat in savasana, in the way that they hold their body during resting time. I have worked with clients who, for many reasons, do not tolerate being in the quiet resting practice in lying down, so I change it. I ask them to move into a supported seated position on a rolled-up blanket on the mat or even to get up off the floor to sit quietly in a supportive chair. There are many reasons for this intolerance to being still that my client may not be ready to share with me. Some of the reasons indicate that my client may benefit from the support of a counselor or trained mental health expert. Because I am not a licensed mental health professional, when it is indicated, I will encourage my client to seek mental health support with a counselor or trained expert. This benefits my client on multiple levels and usually has a positive impact on their therapeutic yoga practices.

CHAPTER 5

WEEK FOUR: IT'S NOT ALWAYS COMFORTABLE

Caroline was sitting on an outdoor chair on her front porch removing her walking shoes and sliding her feet into warm slippers when I arrived at her home for our fourth session. She looked up at me and beamed, "It was such a nice day today, so I decided to go for a short walk this morning before our session. I've been walking every day for about 10 minutes since last week."

"This is great to hear, Caroline. You're looking good. Today, we will review last week's practice and add some stretches that will complement your walking program."

We walked into the house and moved back into the fitness room where Caroline arranged her yoga mat and strap. She reached for her pillows, laughed, and said, "My husband got a kick out of the fact that our throw pillows have a purpose now. Although he joked with me about worrying that this means that I will be getting more of them."

I laughed with her and replied, "Throw pillows are our friends."

Caroline started the Therapeutic Sun Salutation©, moved down to the floor to begin the diaphragmatic breathing practice with lengthened exhalation, and then combined the focused attention to breathing during the bridge posture and knees-to-chest stretch.

"Caroline, you're doing great. Let's continue with some new activities."

She smiled and said, "I'm ready."

I asked her to roll over onto her stomach while she kept breathing rhythmically. I noticed Caroline grimace when she reported feeling tension in her low back. "You need some support under your abdomen, Caroline. Let's put that throw pillow back to work."

She nodded in response and joked, "I'm sensing a theme here, throw pillows are in. My husband is not going to let me forget about this." She winced at the beginning of a laugh that we both shared.

Caroline held her breath when I asked her to lift her torso up from the mat so that I could position the throw pillow beneath her abdomen. She sighed and relaxed back down on the pillow, crossing her arms to rest her forehead on the back of her hands, commenting, "Yes, that feels a whole lot better. It feels so good, like I could be here for a while. Why is that?"

I explained that as mobile and strong as our bodies are, some of us fall into habits or postures that make it easy for the muscles to become accustomed to being in a shortened position. This could happen gradually over long periods of time, so gradual that we don't even notice that it is happening. The type of work or daily activities that we participate in regularly can cause this change. Sitting for long periods at a desk and driving or commuting for long periods of time are some of the most common offenders. Some of us are already predisposed to having these shortened muscles. Then there are others, such as competitive athletes and dancers whose passion, livelihood, and profession require them to generate power from the center of their body over the course of many years. The specific training activities that their sport requires and the repetitive nature of training techniques necessary to keep the muscles strong could also mean that they stay in a shortened state. This often opens the door for imbalance in the hip, spine, and other joints in the surrounding area if they are not identified early in their training programs.

I continued, "Caroline, the challenges that you have moving into and staying in certain positions help me to understand which muscles and structures need attention in the program that I'm creating for you. One of the goals of this program is to help you move out of pain and more easily into more efficient movement patterns in the future."

Caroline shifted and asked, "I don't understand why my body has caused me so much pain over the last few years. What caused this?"

"Caroline, it's possible that you're experiencing a combination of factors or events that have led you to the place that caused your back pain and spasm. Based on what I've noticed today and over the last few sessions that we've worked together, I suspect that your deep hip flexor [psoas] muscles are causing a disturbance in your body's ability to move freely. I also suspect that other muscles like your abdominals are being overwhelmed by this and are not able to activate to support you when you need it most, like transitioning into different positions or moving about in your day-to-day activities. This may cause your back muscles [spinal extensors] to come in to try to help you in your daily activities. When these muscles are continually being asked to work, they can get overwhelmed and over-tired. This can cause them to begin to cramp, or spasm, especially when they are doing work that is not originally part of their primary responsibilities."

WHEN THE BODY IS JUST TRYING TO HELP

Caroline lifted her head from her arms, furrowed her brow, and said, "I'm trying to follow you right now, I'm not sure if I understand it completely, but please continue, maybe something will make sense." She moved back to resting her forehead on the back of her arms.

I went on to explain that muscles that are overworked and doing work that is not their primary responsibility have to exert more effort and can get tired more easily, and this can cause them to cramp or spasm. "Often this is one of the ways that the body uses to get you to stop doing 'offensive activities' that it isn't ready for or hasn't been trained for. As the body loses its tolerance for normal daily activities, a person's endurance and functional strength decline. This can become a vicious cycle of pain, dysfunction, and the body tightening and stiffening to stop motion that causes more pain." I asked Caroline to focus her attention on the feeling of her abdomen and torso moving while she was breathing and listening.

I was observing Caroline as she moved into purposeful breath awareness. After a few rounds of inhalations and exhalations, she said, "It makes sense that I have lost some strength in my core over the years, but I've never thought that muscle tightness could be contributing to my problem. Tell me more about what causes my back spasms. I really want to understand."

I continued, "The cycle of pain that causes muscles to spasm can be overwhelming, painful, and scary, especially when it happens around and along the spine. There are so many tiny and very important muscles that make up the structures that support the spine, and they are all layered one upon the other. They function independent of each other and can also work together as a group to perform special functions. When one or a small group of these muscles become injured or overwhelmed, they begin working harder than they are used to, so the other spinal muscles that lie nearby notice this and come in to help. They have good intentions, they want to help, so they begin to contract to get you to stop moving, and when other muscles nearby join in—BAM!—a full-blown back muscle spasm begins. One that is so powerful, scary, and overwhelming that it can take your breath away."

Caroline lifted her head and said, "You don't have to remind me, I don't ever want to go there again."

I noticed that she was moving a bit more freely in the process of lifting her head off her crossed arms while she was lying, supported on her stomach. This was a good sign that she was tolerating the position well. She returned to her resting position, and I continued, "Many of us know of someone who has back pain and spasm. We might have heard a story or read about a horrific outcome of someone who had constant and severe pain and debilitation. We might know of someone who had a back surgery to help fix pain that went wrong and heard stories about the long-term disability that ensued. When we feel the overwhelming strength of a back spasm, it can make us feel vulnerable, so we ask ourselves whether we are going to stay like this forever, unable to move, work, function, or live life without pain. This loss of control can be overwhelming to anyone. It can be even more overwhelming to someone who has other humans who depend upon them for nurturing, care, and/or other responsibilities. Having to consider how to function and meet the demands of life can be even more frustrating and scary when you must do it with overwhelming back pain and spasm. Questions begin to arise in our minds, 'Who am I if I can't control this? I don't have time for this.' I could go on, and on."

Caroline had been lying on her stomach supported by the pillows for about five minutes during our "learning time." I encouraged her to move out of the position on her abdomen. "Okay, Caroline, it is time to change positions. Keep breathing. Come up onto your elbows, press your forearms and the front of your thighs into the mat, and use the strength of your arms and thighs to help you lift off the pillow. Now lift your hips up, stretch your torso, and sit your bottom back in the direction of your feet. Point your toes so that your ankles extend back behind you. Rest your forehead on your crossed forearms. Feel the stretch at the front of your thighs, and along your spine and torso. Just breathe here in this position for a moment."

She responded with a sigh. "This feels good on my spine and hips, but my feet, my goodness, my toes are cramping. How do I make it stop? I encouraged her to lift her toes to move them in the opposite direction that they were pointed. She repositioned her feet as instructed and found relief.

I continued by sharing, "The cramps in your feet and ankles are like the spasms in your spine. When muscles are doing something that is unfamiliar or that they are not prepared to do, they get overwhelmed, over-tired, and they cramp. It really is that simple. And, yes, it can be surprisingly uncomfortable, even downright painful. And I know that you know this. The good news is, there are ways to reduce their occurrence and possibly make the cramps go away. While it is true, if we make the muscles too tired again, the cramps can come back, but I believe knowing what is causing them takes the mystery and potential fear out of the equation and can make them more tolerable or at least somewhat avoidable. Knowledge is POWER!"

Caroline nodded in agreement and said, "I never thought about what makes the spasms happen. I just know that I don't want them to come back, ever."

"That's enough for today. Go ahead and roll over onto your spine and practice a few more relaxing breaths. Inhale, two, three, four, exhale, two, three, four." I continued to pattern Caroline's breathing for the next 10 breaths while she rested.

"Take your time rolling onto your side to come into the hands and knees and then the downward-facing dog position while you breathe. Now walk your hands towards your feet, keep your legs wide, and come up to standing."

Caroline was moving with purpose and keeping her breathing smooth when she stood up. Things were getting easier. We moved to the front room to review our work for the day and the upcoming homework program that I would be issuing for the next week.

REVIEW OF THE FIRST FOUR SESSIONS AND THE "PERFECT STORM"

"Caroline, the past few sessions have confirmed some of the things that I was suspecting about your situation and the possible source of your back spasms."

Caroline looked surprised and said, "Tell me more about what you see."

I continued, "I've found that your torso is lacking in its ability to reflexively activate your core stabilizing muscles that are supposed to support your body when you are moving from one position to another. This is compounded by a two-inch wide separation in your abdominal muscles. In English this means that you have a weak and potentially unstable core. Your body is trying but hasn't been successful at supporting you to its best abilities."

Caroline asked, "Is this bad? No one ever told me about this."

I continued, "It is a common occurrence for some individuals to have a half-inch to one-inch separation of the abdominal muscles, and that can be normal. Two inches or greater can reflect instability in the torso and core muscle activators, and is cause for concern."

Caroline held her breath. I asked her to breathe and continued to explain that this finding made sense when combined with the difficulty that she had in engaging her abdominals when I asked her to lengthen her exhalation during our first session. This, coupled with the tightness in her deep hip flexor muscles, seems to have created the "perfect storm."

I shared my hypothesis that these things happening at the same time could be responsible for the instability that made her back go out so often over the last year. Caroline's body was doing the best that it could but was overwhelmed by a lack of coordination, reduced muscular strength and endurance, and reduced activation of the core stabilizing muscles that were not able to do their intended job. This put the burden on other muscles that were able to help her but were not designed to do this work on a regular basis. These muscles got tired and would spasm. Caroline's hip flexors had gotten very comfortable with being in a shortened state over the years. She had spent a lot of time sitting at her desk for hours at her job, driving for extended periods in her car for her work, and driving her children to activities in the after-school hours. It was possible that she had missed an opportunity to bring these tight muscles closer to balance when she skipped stretching her body at the end of her running and fitness training. Her body was just responding to what it was experiencing. The strong hip flexors were taking over. They were getting stronger and tighter over the years, making the imbalance worse, encouraging, and then continuing the cycle of spasm and pain.

A Note About Diastasis Recti

I referred to Caroline not demonstrating the automatic reflexive activation of her core muscles and that she presented with a two-inch separation of her rectus abdominal muscle. In the clinic, we often measure and then document this by referring to finger widths. I would place my finger(s) in the depressed area of the separation (see illustration). A three-finger width separation (a diastasis recti) is not normal but is often a common occurrence for individuals who are deconditioned, have been through a pregnancy, are obese, or have a large protruding abdomen that puts pressure on the abdominal muscles and overstretches them. During the session with Caroline, I recognized that the separation of her abdominals might be contributing to if not the source of her back problems. Up to that time, I had not had a client present with this amount of weakness and instability, but I understood how it could happen. I had my own personal experience with this.

Diastasis recti is an increased distance between the rectus abdominis muscles at the midline caused by weakness in the anterior abdominal wall. Most experts agree that there is a weakness, thinning, and widening of the linea alba and weakness of the associated abdominal musculature.

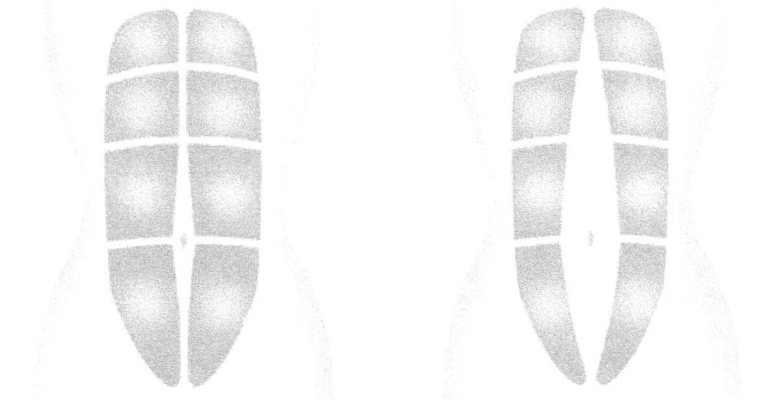

I did recognize the uncoordinated abdominal muscles from my own personal experience, directly after the birth of my first child. I had returned from the hospital and was back at my own home just a few days postpartum. I went to the bathroom to empty my bladder. Who would have known that such a normal human function could become such an adventure? If you have experienced a vaginal delivery resulting in an episiotomy, you will understand what I am referring to. But that is a whole other story. I positioned my-

self to sit on the toilet, and as soon as I sat down, a wave of fear or uncertainty (that's the best way that I can describe it) moved through me. Something didn't feel right when I was in the "sitting on the toilet" position. I called out to my husband who was in the living room with the baby. "Something doesn't feel right." I realized that the odd sensation that my whole body was sensing was a complete lack of being able to activate my abdominals to stabilize my body while sitting on the toilet. You may not be aware, but research has found that the slouched posture that is regularly assumed when sitting on a standard Western toilet creates an intense amount of pressure on the discs in the lumbar spine. The Western toilet sitting position is known to significantly increase intra disc pressure in the lumbar spine.

My abdominals had been stretched to the extreme during my pregnancy, and then they were tested to their limits when they had endured the rigors of six hours of hard labor. Talk about stress to the structures. My body recognized the instability and was doing everything in its limited power at that time to help me, but it was at a severe disadvantage in that particular sitting position. My husband had to help me get back up off the toilet.

I was surprised, but my experience made perfect sense. When I checked my own body, I presented with a four-finger width separation of my abdominals. This finding made sense due to the stress of the whole pregnancy and vaginal delivery ordeal. I had a flashback of recall from postgraduate spine continuing education courses that reported about the seat on the standard Western-designed toilet position being the most stressful to the lumbar disc structures. Yikes! When I called out to my husband, it was because the sensation of instability was so unsettling, something I was not used to in my life's work and practice of not only guiding others in improving and/or maintaining core fitness and functional mobility but also practicing it myself. The feeling made me a bit queasy. Possibly because I was overwhelmed with fear of the unknown. How long would this sensation last? I couldn't get up off the toilet. Would I be stuck there forever? My usual independent personality needed help and in the most vulnerable (on the toilet) situation. Fortunately for me, my husband is also a physical therapist, and we had both been very used to helping our patients off the toilet, and it wasn't like he didn't know that I pooped and peed on occasion. Ha!

That humbling event gave me a whole new appreciation for what my clients were experiencing when they suffered back pain due to core discoordination and instability. I never have forgotten that ex-

perience. It guides me to this day when I am helping my patients and clients move through spine conditions.

Caroline was not able to generate the automatic and reflexive activation of her abdominals during the activities that I asked her to perform when she was lying down on the mat. She had reported feeling pressure in her low back and feeling unsteady in her attempt at the therapeutic bridge pose. She tired easily and was unable to co-contract and activate her abdominal muscles when I guided her with verbal cues in activities that would have (under normal conditions) resulted in an active contraction. I knew then that the likely source of her problem was core abdominal discoordination and lack of reflexive activation. It made perfect sense to me why her back "went out," why it was lasting so long when it was out, and why it was occurring so frequently. I explained my hypothesis to Caroline, the ideas behind the instability connection to her frequent bouts of back pain and shared that I had a plan of action for her. At this point, after having suffered so long, she was ready to try anything that might help her recover her active lifestyle and freedom from back pain.

Caroline exclaimed, "Wow, all this time I've been upset at my body because of my back spasms, I didn't know that my muscles were just trying to help me."

I continued, "We humans have been designed extremely well. There's no accident about every part of us. And each part is designed to influence and affect every other part. We are truly amazing. So much, that it surprises us when things aren't working as intended and we begin to break down."

Caroline asked, "Is there anything that I can do? Will I be able to make this better?"

I responded, "Yes, your program has started you on the path to improving your core strength and stability. You are doing well with these beginning activities. We will continue to build your therapeutic yoga practice over the next few weeks to help you have a well-rounded program that helps you address the areas in question. So far, you are doing very well. I hope that you are noticing a subtle improvement. Next week, I will guide you in some activities that will continue to balance your program."

I reached into my files and collected the sheets that reflected the activities that we added during that session, "Caroline, you will work on balancing your hip flexor and spine muscles when you lie on your stomach with a small pillow under your abdomen for 20 to 40 breaths. Take rest by moving onto your side to lie with a pillow between your legs for 10 breaths, and then move into the most comfortable expression of child's pose that works for you. Add this to your program."

Caroline said, "My list of activities is growing. I think that I am going to like the child's pose a lot."

"You can move into the most comfortable postures that you prefer at any time to help you find tension relief during your day. You should be proud. You are making steady progress," I said, as I handed Caroline the printed program.

Caroline responded, "I can feel the benefits happening already, just in the way that I'm moving down onto the floor. I'm happy that my therapeutic yoga practice is helping me feel a little bit better every day."

We moved out of the fitness room, and walking to the front door, I said, "Okay, Caroline, keep working on your therapeutic yoga practice so that you will be ready to continue our adventures next week."

Caroline walked with me to the door, and we said our goodbyes.

I settled into my car to take a few minutes to make notes in my files of the session that had just ended. I was pleased with the gradual progress that Caroline was making. Barring any unforeseen circumstances, she was on the way to experiencing significant improvements in her whole function, strength, and range of motion. I started the engine and continued to my next appointment.

A Structured Sequence: Repetition Can Have Its Advantages

Caroline was doing well with her program. I could see her progress with each follow-up visit that I made. She was able to demonstrate each posture with only a few reminders to watch her breath and minor positioning changes. She was getting stronger, but still needed more time and consistent work. The separation of her abdominals was reducing gradually, and her ability to automatically activate her core stabilizers was improving. This was a great sign of her continuing progress. Caroline was on the way to reducing the instability that caused her spine muscles to spasm. Time and her continued consistent effort would benefit her.

At this point, the benefits of the structured sequence become apparent. I have taken advantage of using a structured sequence of activities in program development with my physical therapy patients and therapeutic yoga clients over the years. It is standard practice to create a structured program of exercise based on the results of the clinical assessment that I had performed of my patient's physical and functional status. Using a structured sequence of exercise helps to develop a solid foundation to build upon a patient's strengths while being mindful of their limitations. The repetition of the structured sequence as it is being developed helps to create new patterns of movement that will benefit the patient in their continued progress towards improved functional mobility.

Years ago, when I began to incorporate the physical practices of yoga into my physical therapy treatments, this blending of approaches then seeped back into the therapeutic yoga that I was developing for my personal practice. Over time, it positively influenced my work with my therapeutic yoga clients. The structured sequences showed up again when I began to read about, study, and then practice the primary series of the Ashtanga yoga lineage. I had already been creating variations of the traditional Hatha yoga postures before I was introduced to the Ashtanga lineage in the writings of Beryl's book, Power Yoga. *I continued making modifications as I needed them and used the repetition of performing the postures in the structured sequence to monitor my personal progress. It was a success. I was able to see the slight changes that were taking place in my body and how it was tolerating the more vigorous practice.*

Why I appreciate using a structured sequence:

1. Using a structured sequence helped me to have a template to measure my own progress in my personal practice. Over time, I was able to use structured sequences to monitor clients' progress in their programs.
2. The repetition helps the client learn the sequence. The more often that they repeat the movements in the specific sequence, the easier it becomes to move from one posture to the other.
3. The repetition helps to more easily identify limitations or areas that need more attention.
4. Repeating a structured sequence can help to build a solid foundation for functional movements that can be progressed by adding other activities that are more challenging over time.

5. Repeating a structured sequence can be helpful when it is necessary to step the intensity of a practice down to meet the needs of a temporary setback.

This is where the scientist comes out in me within the work that I have been doing developing the therapeutic yoga practices that I share with my clients. I use the postures to address the limitations and build upon them as the client progresses in strength, range of motion, endurance, and functional mobility. It has been an extension of the integrative work that I have done in the physical therapy practices that I have created over the years.

Progress in the practice often means adding a few more postures. You must do the work to make change.

A month had passed, and Caroline had four weeks of practice under her belt. She was showing gradual but consistent improvement in her ability to tolerate and execute the activities in her therapeutic yoga program. Caroline was practicing every day on her own for at least 30 minutes in each session. Our visits lasted for an hour. She would demonstrate her practice and ask any questions about her program. I would give her feedback and any instructions that might encourage her success in the practices.

The follow-up sessions serve many purposes, and each time that I see a client, I can assess their progress, add or subtract a posture, or make variations to the existing program. It is obvious when a client is not doing their daily therapeutic yoga practice. I can usually tell by the way that the client has difficulty looking me in the eye when I ask how their practice is coming along. But even if the client tells me a bold-faced lie about doing their work, their body never lies. It is apparent that they have not done the work because they do not make progress. When something like this comes up in a private session, I will have a direct conversation with the client. I always want them to know that they are ultimately responsible for their return to wellness and that it will take work.

This was not the case with Caroline. I could see subtle changes in the way that she was moving from one position to the other. Her movements were improving in their coordination, and her strength was gradually increasing. This showed itself when she did the Therapeutic Sun Salutation©. This is another reason for using it with my clients: It is an excellent tool for measuring functional progress. Caroline was ready for more. It was time to progress forward and add the rest of her therapeutic yoga practices to complete her program.

The Little Things That We Often Take for Granted

I often find that it is easy for us to take the things that we do in our daily lives for granted. Standing, walking, being able to lie down, get up, lie on our stomachs, sides, etc. To just perform what seem like basic activities of daily living. We take them for granted and often don't appreciate them until they are challenged. The therapeutic yoga practices that I develop are aimed at taking basic functions of daily life and working to improve our ability to perform them. These practices are aimed towards making living easier so that we might be able to enjoy it better.

CHAPTER 6

WEEK SIX: DOING THE WORK. WALKING THE WALK

Caroline opened the front door and invited me into her home. We walked back towards the fitness room. Caroline's mobility and strength were improving. At Week Six, it was apparent that she had been consistent and persistent in her walking program and home therapeutic yoga practice. She moved through the Therapeutic Sun Salutation© with ease and talked about how much she was enjoying her outdoor walking program. "I'm so happy that I'm walking in the neighborhood again. I gradually increased my time, and now I'm walking for 20 minutes. I'm so happy to be able to enjoy the outdoors again. It's becoming an important part of my day." Caroline focused her attention on keeping her breath smooth during her movements down to the floor and then back up. It was obvious that she was doing the work.

"Caroline, your body is telling on you."

She grimaced and asked nervously, "What do you mean by that?"

I smiled and said, "Don't worry. What I mean is that I can see the progress that you're making. It's obvious that you've been doing your homework."

Caroline looked relieved and said, "My body better not be telling you that I haven't been doing the work because I will have to have a talk with her."

We both laughed and I continued, "Today, we're going to spend most of our time working on some new postures. These postures will add mobility and flexibility while continuing to work on improving the strength and endurance of your body."

Caroline's face brightened, and she exclaimed, "I'm ready. Bring it on!"

Caroline stretched her arms up, moved into a squat, set her hands down onto her yoga mat, stretched back into a downward-facing dog, and held it for a few breaths before bending her knees to settle into a child's pose with her forearms crossed beneath her forehead. "Do you know that I really like this position? It just feels good to be able to get down on the floor. I feel like a kid when I do this. I remember when we first did this, and it wasn't so easy."

I moved to sit on the floor beside her and shared, "I'm so encouraged by the work that you're doing. It's making a difference. These next activities will complement the work that you've already begun."

ATTENTION TO THE BREATH AND YOUR POSITION CAN MAKE A DIFFERENCE

Caroline moved onto her back where I began to guide her into practicing the supine single-knee-to-chest stretch. She held the position for five breaths before I asked her to move her thigh across her body to encourage a hip stretch with a gentle spinal twist. "It's important to keep breathing while you focus on keeping your right shoulder on the mat when you stretch your right thigh across your body in this posture. This will help you know how far to move into the spinal twist. If your breathing gets short or if your right shoulder comes off the mat, you know that you are doing more than necessary. Go ahead and turn your head to the right, to look over your right shoulder."

Caroline moved carefully into the spinal twist, listening to every cue that I offered. She noticed when her breath started to change as she reached the maximum twist in her body. "I understand what you mean about keeping my shoulder down and watching my breathing. I can really feel the change when I go too far in this posture." Caroline moved back to center and repeated the activity on the left side.

I replied, "This is a good observation. These subtle changes are made more apparent when we focus our attention on our breath." I reached for her yoga strap, handed it to Caroline, and guided her into the supine hamstring stretch with strap. She held this for 10 breaths on each side and then came into resting position, lying on her back with her knees bent.

"I really felt that stretch behind my lower ankle when I placed the strap at the ball of my foot like you asked. I didn't notice it as much when I first started. I thought that you said I would feel this at the back of my thigh."

I could see the look of curiosity forming on Caroline's face, and I responded, "Each person will feel the effect of the stretch positions in different places, depending on the past experiences of their bodies. Currently, many of us spend a lot more time sitting than we've ever done so as a species. Our lifestyle, work habits, and the myriad of technological advances have encouraged us to be more sedentary than ever before. This has influenced the balance of muscle strength, flexibility, and mobility that we experience in our bodies. The back of the thigh [hamstrings] and lower leg [calf] muscles get used to being in a shortened state when we sit a lot, and they get tight."

Caroline responded, "I realize now that I became less active when I started working in real estate. I really loved working with my clients, learning about the business, and helping people navigate selling and buying a home. It made me happy to see my clients find their dream homes. I threw myself into my work and didn't notice that I stopped my regular exercise program, and now that I think about it, I really did sit for a lot longer than ever before. I was driving a lot more and spending more time at my desk in the office."

I reached for the stretch strap, handed it back to Caroline, and said, "Let's do the hamstring stretch again. This time you will hold it for five breaths because we are going to add some movements to stretch your inner thigh [hip adductor] and outer thigh [hip abductor] muscles."

Caroline, following my verbal cues, started with the right thigh, holding each position for five breaths. I asked her to keep her hips level on the mat when she took the strap into her left hand and began to move her right thigh slowly across her body.

"I want you to listen carefully to your breath in this important posture. We start with your hips even on the mat for the first five breaths. If you feel comfortable and your breath remains smooth, then you can allow your right thigh to move further to your left side. And if this feels good, you can allow your right hip to come off the mat."

Caroline moved slowly, maintaining the fullness of her soft breathing when her hips were evenly supported on the mat. Her breath began to get rough as she started to lift her right hip off the mat when her right thigh tried to move across her body to the left side. She held her breath. "Ouch! I'm not sure about this stretch. I can feel it in my back and not in a good way." She moved her right leg back to the beginning position.

"Good catch, Caroline. You're listening to your body, and it's letting you know that you aren't ready for the movement across your body on this side right now. Keep breathing. Let's try the other side."

Caroline repeated the activities on the left side. She moved carefully when it came time to cross her left thigh over towards the right side. Her left hip was able to elevate about an inch off the mat. "I feel the stretch, and I'm breathing, but I think I'll stay right here for this stretch. I don't want to go any further right now." Caroline moved back to the midline position and slowly lowered her left leg back to the resting supported position.

"Good call, Caroline. Just do as much of the stretch as you are comfortable with. You'll have plenty of time to expand on this posture in the future. You're doing well to listen to your body."

I asked Caroline to roll onto her stomach to hold prone extension on a small pillow for 10 breaths. "Lift your chest and torso and come up onto your elbows. Breathe." Caroline was able to keep her breathing steady during the challenge of lifting her torso from the pillow. This was a good sign. I took the opportunity to remove the pillow from beneath her abdomen. Caroline followed my cues and moved back down onto the mat, lying flat on her abdomen, and held the position easily for 10 breaths.

"Caroline, you are progressing well with the spine and hip extension in this posture. Your practice is showing the benefits to your whole-body mobility." I invited her to move back into child's pose to allow her spine and the back of her hips to stretch. She held the position for 10 breaths, then moved onto her hands and knees, and allowed me to guide her through the rest of the quadruped postures before ending in the downward-facing dog. She moved into resting position on her spine.

Use the Breath to Monitor the Intensity of the Work. Use the Breath to Know When You Need to Take Rest

In this session, Caroline had several experiences of noticing how her breath was able to help her know when she was in a position that her body was not ready for. This is an important awareness process that will help an individual take care of their physical body when approaching activities in exercise and daily living. This awareness can help reduce overworking and might possibly reduce their having a "setback" in their functional progress towards well-being.

A Note About the Hamstring Stretch With Strap

We added the back of the thigh (hamstring) stretches, which is a posture that I call the supine hamstring stretch. I always encourage my clients to use a non-stretch strap to help support the body while performing the therapeutic yoga practices. In this case, the strap is looped around the ball of the foot for the leg that is being stretched. This allows a bonus of stretching the whole back of the thigh and the lower leg muscles too. Many of us know that our hamstrings are tight, but we don't often realize that the muscular tightness often extends along the whole backside of the body, down to the feet. A non-stretch strap offers the practitioner a stable support that can encourage the nervous system to trust the stretch that is being placed on the muscles. I have found that this can make a significant impact on improving the results of an individual's efforts for their practice.

The addition of stretch to the inner and outer thighs (hip adductor and hip abductor muscles) is also important for helping a person come back to balance when they have had spine pain. We don't often realize how the muscle tightness in the lower body impacts the pelvis, which is intimately connected to the spine via muscle, connective tissue, fascia, and bony joints. Keeping the muscles strong and mobile goes a long way towards helping improve a person's quality of life and functional capacity.

The straight leg stretch, where we move the thigh across to the opposite side of the body, is a challenging practice that must be done with awareness. The long lever that the thigh creates can pull a lot of tension on the spinal muscles and connective tissue that have to stabilize the torso. It is not uncommon for individuals with core instability to feel uncomfortable with this activity. For this reason, I encourage slow, gentle, breath-centered progression.

A Note About Reciprocal Inhibition

[Isometric Quadricep Activation and Reciprocal Inhibition of the Hamstring Muscles]

During the practice of the hamstring stretch with strap, I cue the client to begin to straighten the knee as much as possible and to engage the front of both thighs to perform a contraction of the quadriceps muscle. This activation of the quadricep is designed to activate automatic reflexes in the nervous system to encourage relaxation in the hamstring muscle that is being stretched. I usually share the reason behind this request in a story like this:

"When you purposefully engage the front of the thigh [quadriceps] muscle, your nervous system notices and sends a message to the brain that the quadriceps are 'working' to straighten the knee (because that is their job). This stimulates an automatic reflex that causes a release of tension in the hamstring muscle. The hamstring muscle is effectively encouraged to relax [reciprocal inhibition]. This helps the quadriceps muscles increase their ability to contract and can improve strength over time. The relaxed hamstrings can improve their flexibility over time. When we repeat the stretches with this activation and relaxation over time, the physiology of the muscles is altered with the end result of lengthened hamstrings and strengthened quadriceps. This can lead to improved balance of the knee joint with an improved length/tension relationship to improve mechanical function of the joint."

Straightening the knee is not as easy as it sounds in this position because the hamstrings are often tight. When hamstring tightness is allowed to continue without intervention, this can cause inhibition of the quadriceps (making them weaker) and can continue to contribute to an imbalance in the strength/tension relationship along the knee joint that can become the onset of knee instability.

This type of reciprocal inhibition can be encouraged along any joint in the body. We activate muscles on one side of a joint to inhibit the muscles on the opposite side. Another example is the engagement of the gluteal muscles at the back of the hip to help encourage a release of the deep hip flexors muscles that influence the front of the hip.

This form of mindful awareness to activating and strengthening muscles that help to relax and lengthen opposite muscles can influence the major joints of the body and bring them closer to anatomical balance and possibly away from stress and dysfunction.

It makes active stretching a process where active strengthening is happening, and the result can be that the major joints that are affected can benefit from becoming more balanced over the long term. This is a fundamental principle that lies at the foundation of the Therapeutic Astanga Method©.

CHAPTER **7**

WEEK EIGHT: REPEAT THE OFFENSIVE ACTIVITIES

Caroline reported feeling more comfortable during her 20-minute morning walking program as she opened her front door to let me in. "I can feel the muscles in my legs getting stronger every day. It feels good to feel strong again and not have back pain. I've not had a muscle spasm during the time that I've been doing my therapeutic yoga practices. I've felt some of my muscles get tired, but no back spasms. I hope that they're gone for good."

We moved into the fitness room where Caroline started her practice of the Therapeutic Sun Salutation©. She moved into downward-facing dog, then child's pose. At the end of child's pose, I guided her through the quadruped, thread the needle, and then back to child's pose.

"I like the way that I'm moving from one posture to the next. The cat/cow stretch feels good, I remember doing something like this years ago in a fitness class. It's like I'm going back in time."

I nodded and shared, "Therapeutic yoga can have that effect on the body. It can make it feel stronger, more mobile, and can help us move through our day with less effort. I'm glad to know that you're feeling good in your practice."

FEELING GOOD TAKES EFFORT

"If I'm being completely honest with you," Caroline said, "I'm not always excited to start doing my therapeutic yoga practice on my own, especially now that I'm feeling better. I have days when I can think of so many other things to do instead of my therapeutic yoga practice."

89

"Oh, Caroline, you're not alone. You've just shared one of the most common challenges that many of us experience when starting a new program. It can be exciting at first, especially when it involves improving our health. In the first few months, it seems to be easy to stay on track when we're seeing and feeling the results of our consistent effort. We begin to experience improvement in our ability to perform daily living activities. We feel better, we sleep better, and it impacts everything in our lives for the better. After some time, we stop noticing the improvement in our functioning, as if it falls into the background. We forget that it's our continued activity that influences our endurance, strength, and mobility, and keeps us pain-free and functional."

Caroline nodded, "What I'm feeling now is the opposite of my experiences during the months when my back would go out. I never knew what started them. Looking back at it now, I guess they came on when I was really stressed. I just remember that I would have strong spasms that would kick in whenever I tried to move. I couldn't get out of bed. I used to take pain medicine for this, and it worked just enough to help me get to the bathroom, but it was still excruciating. I didn't do much during those episodes, and after a while they began to last longer and started to occur more frequently. My husband didn't know how to help me. I was so tired of hurting, feeling foggy from the pain medication, and not being able to have an active life. I didn't think that I could ever get back to walking outdoors for exercise, much less do the activities that you've shared with me. I'm happy to forget about the pain."

"It's a good thing that we can forget what it felt like when we were deconditioned, in pain, or limited in our functional ability. Our nervous system experiences these pain events as traumatic episodes in our life and has mechanisms in place that protect and help us cope by reducing our memory of them. At the same time, I believe that our forgetting what got us into trouble in the first place and the pain that we felt at the time can make slipping back into old habits more common. We start feeling better when we're doing the work that improves our state of health and functional mobility, and we begin to forget that our consistent effort in our program is what is behind that feeling. Little things begin to interfere with our practice, and before we know it, we stop doing it altogether. If this continues, we slowly start to feel the fatigue, pain, or dysfunction that we started with, and sometimes it is even more painful than before."

Caroline looked worried. "I NEVER want to feel like I did when my back was in full spasm. It was the worst! I'm glad that I've scheduled my therapeutic yoga practice on my daily schedule. I may not always want to do it, but after I'm done, I always feel better and am glad that I did."

I responded, "You and me alike, Caroline. I do the same thing. My personal therapeutic yoga practice is on my permanent mental calendar. It is part of my personal habits like eating, sleeping, and grooming. I don't feel quite the same when I don't do it. Thank you for sharing this with me. Once again, I want to remind you that you are not alone; we are a team."

I guided Caroline as she continued with her program, moving through the therapeutic bridge pose, then the knees-to-chest stretch before rolling over to lie completely flat on her abdomen in prone extension. I took the opportunity to ask her to move up onto her elbows, up into a moment of hyperextension of her spine, into the sphinx posture. She held it for five breaths and then moved back down to rest on her abdomen for 10 breaths.

"In our last session, we talked about the effect of reduced activity and more sitting on your body, specifically the hamstring muscles at the back of your thighs. There are some other very important muscles that can get tight that are not as popular, and many people have no idea they even exist."

Caroline responded, "When I considered beginning a therapeutic yoga program with you, I had no idea that I would be learning so much about my body and the different muscles that I have. I can't always remember the names, but I remember where they are when I'm strengthening and stretching them. I like this learning."

I smiled and said, "This is good to hear. I want to make certain that I'm not overwhelming you with too much information. On that note, let me tell you a little about how sitting for longer periods can also influence the strong hip flexor and rotator muscles at the hip joints. This a great segue for the next postures."

Caroline sighed, "I knew that I should have kept my thoughts to myself." She smiled, "Just kidding, what else do you have for me?"

I guided her through the supine hip rotation postures and then the supine figure-four stretch posture. I encouraged her to hold each posture for five breaths on each side. She did each posture well, so I added an extra stretch to the figure-four position. I handed Caroline her strap and showed her how to loop it around her thigh.

I continued, "Caroline, we're using the strap to help support your thigh in the elevated portion of this figure-four stretch. This posture is excellent for helping us recognize how tightness in the hips, thighs, and lower body can influence the whole back of the body, moving all the way up to the neck and head. I want you to pay special attention to the position of your head and neck, as well as your breath, when you do this stretch. The muscles that connect your shoulder blades to your rib cage [in the scapulo-thoracic junction] will play an important role in helping you to stabilize your neck and head when you are in this position. Using the yoga strap will make it easier for you to support your spine and to be successful in this position. Over time, you may notice that you won't need the strap. That is another way that we will measure progress."

Caroline shared, "I can really feel this stretch in my butt and lower back. It feels good to get a stretch there." She held the position for 10 breaths and then repeated it on the other side before returning to resting on her spine with her knees bent and feet on the mat.

We were nearing the end of the practice, so I guided Caroline into a gentle spine twist while she rested on her spine. This is one of my favorite postures that encourages a gentle massage of the internal organs and a lengthening of the muscles along the sides of the torso and spine.

Caroline shared, "This stretch feels a lot like the knee-to-chest stretch with a twist, and yet it feels different somehow. It almost feels gentler, but maybe that's because I am starting to pay closer attention to this whole yoga breathing and movement thing. I can actually feel how it challenges my ability to breathe smoothly, but it feels good at the same time. I used to be afraid of doing movements like this when I had my back spasms, but now it just feels like the right thing to do."

"Caroline, you are doing well in this work towards improving your mindful awareness of what your body, mind, and spirit need. I am very encouraged to hear you share this with me. I believe that this awareness will carry over into many of the other parts of your life. This is just the beginning of what can be a great skill to take forward to support your long-term wellbeing."

Little Things Can Make a Big Difference

The hip rotation activities that I shared with Caroline were designed to influence the mobility and strength of the rotator muscles in her hips. Unless you make a living and have committed your life and passion to understanding and studying the physiology of the body, you may not realize that these are very important muscles that influence the mobility, strength, and stability of your hips. They are easy to overlook because these muscles are relatively small when you compare them to the large muscles of your thighs and buttocks. These "little muscles" exert a lot of influence on the hip joint. I have found that when they are not cared for or given the attention that they require (to maintain their strength and flexibility) that they are often responsible for creating the restrictions in the hip joint that then begin to negatively impact the knee joint below and the spine and pelvic segments above.

The hip rotation activities included hip internal and external rotation stretches that Caroline would do lying on her back (in the supine position) and the supine figure-four posture with a strap for support. These movement activities would be sufficient to begin the process of mobilizing the hips gently to help us know what restrictions might exist. We would use the same activities to begin strengthening and stretching the rotator muscles to help them return to as close to balance as possible.

The gentle spine twist activity that I shared with Caroline near the end of her practice is one of the most popular stretches that I share with my therapeutic yoga students and physical therapy patients. Most every person that I know with spine pain does some form of this gentle twist. I always like to make sure that my client is moving mindfully and focusing their attention on maintaining smooth and gentle breathing during the activity to make certain that they are not pushing too hard. That is the beauty of these mindful, breath-centered awareness practices—if we pay attention to how our breath is flowing during the movement, we will always know how much effort to produce. At the end of the day, we want our nervous system to trust that the movements and activities that we are doing are going to help us move forward with greater ease and less discomfort.

GETTING UPSIDE DOWN

I reached for the throw pillows that Caroline had in the fitness room and stated, "And now for one of my favorite postures. I hope that you appreciate this posture as much as I do. It's called the supported legs-up-the-wall posture. It is an accessible variation to the legs-up-the-wall posture where we don't even need to have a wall. A few pillows will do."

Caroline smiled and said, "Let's hear it for my throw pillow friends. I was beginning to miss them since I stopped using them under my belly for my stretching, but I kept them here just in case I needed them."

I guided Caroline into position where she was lying on her spine with her knees bent then asked her to elevate her hips as if to perform a therapeutic bridge posture. I placed the two flat pillows under her pelvis before asking her to lower her hips to rest them on the pillows and asked, "Does that feel comfortable?"

Caroline responded, "Yes, I can feel a stretch in my low back. It feels good."

I continued, "Okay, Caroline, keep breathing while you lift your right foot off the floor to invite your right knee towards your chest and hold it there. If that feels okay, then lift your left foot and invite your left knee to join your right. Hold in this position, feel the stretch. It should feel good. Keep breathing."

She held the position for three breaths.

"If that feels good, go ahead and begin to straighten your right knee so that your leg is stretching straight up to the ceiling and follow with your left side." Caroline maintained her focused concentration on every word that I shared while keeping her breath rhythmic and steady.

"This position should be easy to maintain. We use the pillows to elevate your hips so that once your legs are elevated, you should not have to work hard to keep them up in the position." Caroline was doing well. Her legs stayed vertical while she rested in the position.

"This is a perfect place to practice your ankle and foot mobility activities." I guided her through large ankle circles in both directions, beginning with her toes flexed and then progressing to the movements with her toes extended. I noticed that Caroline was holding her breath during the foot and ankle movements and reminded her to keep breathing.

"I didn't even notice that I was holding my breath. I was trying to do the activities as you were leading me. There's a lot more to these foot and ankle activities than I realized. I never knew that my ankles could get so tired."

At the end of this work, I guided Caroline to bend her knees and slowly lower one leg at a time so that she could place her feet on the mat and lift her hips to remove the pillows. I placed a small pillow behind Caroline's knees and said, "Take rest," and for the next five minutes, I allowed Caroline to lie with her eyes closed on her yoga mat for an important part of the therapeutic yoga practice. The resting practice. This part of the practice is as important as the physical activities that we do to strengthen, lengthen, or stabilize the body. I mentioned earlier that this is where we allow the body to rest and to return to a balanced state. This part of the practice reminds us of the importance of keeping our attention on the benefits that come to the mind, body, and spirit when we value rest as much as we value hard work. This is also a time when I sit quietly with my client and reflect upon the practice that I shared for that session. I am in a quiet observation mode to make sure that my client is comfortable and tolerating the resting position well.

At the end of the five-minute rest period, I invited Caroline to move out of the resting practice and slowly back up into the seated position on the mat. Caroline shared, "Wow, I feel very relaxed. I almost fell asleep right now."

"This is good to hear, Caroline. It's nice to see that you can relax into the resting position easily at the end of your practice. You did great work today." I reached into my files to find copies of the new postures that we added to the program for that day. "Here are your new therapeutic yoga practices. You have a solid program that's mobilizing every major joint of your body in a gentle way."

Caroline said, "I think that I'll be feeling these new activities. It felt good to get the stretch in my lower body and hips. I hope that I'm not too sore."

"I don't expect that you will be incapacitated by these new stretches, but you might notice a bit of soreness along the back of your hips, thighs, and lower legs tomorrow. I'll encourage you to repeat these slightly offensive activities with full attention on your breath, so that your nervous system can begin to realize that this will be a normal and regular occurrence in your body."

Caroline laughed and repeated the phrase, "Slightly offensive, oh my!"

We reviewed the addition of the new practices and the process of melding them with her existing activities before we ended our session. Caroline walked me to her front door, and we said our goodbyes. I spent a few minutes making notes in my files before driving out to my next appointment for the day.

Changing Our Perspective—The World Looks Different When You Are Upside Down

The Supine Supported Legs-Up-the-Wall Posture

When it is appropriate, I recommend that a person practice some form of gentle inversion somewhere in their personal therapeutic yoga practice. Caroline's program encouraged this in her practice of the downward-facing dog posture and the supported legs-up-the-wall posture. It has been my experience to notice that everything in the world looks different when we are upside down. Our face even looks different because the pull of gravity is opposite the normal pull when we are standing or sitting right side up.

Of the many benefits that we can achieve from practicing gentle inversions, some of my favorites are that the heart muscle is able to take a "relative" rest when we elevate the legs in the supported legs-up-the-wall posture. When the legs are up in the air, gravity helps the veins deliver blood back to the lungs with greater ease. As the blood continues moving through the circulatory system, oxygen is put back in it. The blood then continues to the heart where it is pumped back to the brain, organs, muscles, and tissues within the body. For this particular action, the heart muscle doesn't have to work against the pull of gravity to get the blood back to the lungs and heart. This is a change from the norm when we are typically upright for most of the day, and this short-term change can be considered a form of rest for the heart. Having the legs up in the air also helps with encouraging the drainage of any excess fluid that might be accumulating in the foot and ankle to circulate back into the body system. This can help improve comfort and healing of any challenges that are occurring in the foot or lower body.

I also like to recommend getting upside down to help interrupt a person's mindset when they are in the middle of a stressful situation. Getting upside down changes our perspective, how we look at things. I have used this process myself over the years when I am overwhelmed, overstimulated, over-tired, or just stuck, fixated on a problem that I am not able to solve. When I recognize my state of mind is stuck and I can't focus anymore, I go find a place where I can get upside down. If I can't get on the floor, then I just sit in a chair and drop my head down as if I am reaching for something on the floor. When I return to the upright position, the blood goes from my head back to the rest of my body and the problem seems to lose its power over me. I have changed my perspective by doing some form of an inversion over the years. I have received inspiration and have solved many problems using this method. At minimum, I got a break from the stress and anxiety that I was feeling. It has helped me many times over the last 40 years.

Precautions for Practicing Variations to Supported Inversions

There are a few people who need to exercise caution when practicing these variations of gentle inversions. You will want to seek the guidance of your medical team to see if getting upside down is right for you if you have a history of or active situation of glaucoma, retinal detachment, uncontrolled high blood pressure, or other condition where you have been advised not to let your head stay below the level of your heart for an extended period of time. There may be temporary conditions that occur in your life where you will avoid getting upside down for a short period. This might include directly after cataract or other eye surgeries, and other medical or surgical treatments that your medical team might advise limiting inversions.

Listen to your instinct. Your gut never lies.

Another important guide to follow that will help you to know when practicing inversions (or any other postures for that matter) is not appropriate is to listen to your gut instinct. If you feel uncomfortable, nervous, anxious, or irritated when beginning to assume a posture or when you are already in a posture, this is a sign from your body that it is not tolerating it well. Allow yourself to move out of the posture and/or find a position that makes you feel more comfortable. Your body has its own wisdom. These therapeutic yoga practices are designed to help you begin to quiet the "noise" and allow you to "hear" this wisdom speak.

Balance and Coordination Depend on Your Foot and Ankle Mobility, Stability, Strength, and Muscular Endurance

Another very important part of Caroline's long-term therapeutic yoga program involved setting a solid foundation of strength, range of motion, stability, and mobility for her feet and ankles. We addressed this in several ways. We began by encouraging awareness of the importance of setting a solid foundation in the standing position on the mat, in bare feet. Making sure that she was aware of the importance of her feet and keeping an awareness of their position in every standing, seated, and lying-down posture. I shared cues with her about keeping an energetic awareness of the feet by engaging the muscles around the foot and ankle. We also did this by implementing basic mindful foot and ankle exercises that she could perform at the end of her therapeutic yoga practice or whenever she had a moment during her day. These activities targeted strengthening every muscle that influenced the natural movements of the ankle and foot in daily living activities and walking. These activities are an excellent way to focus our attention, and they challenge our ability to maintain smooth and rhythmic breathing. Of the programs that I have shared with my clients over the years, the foot and ankle activities are the ones where my clients are focusing so much on trying to do them that they often begin to hold their breath. So much for this being a basic practice. The amount of paying attention necessary to do these activities and maintain smooth breathing can make this practice quite advanced. It is well worth the effort.

The Path Is Not Always Easy

And then there were the times that Caroline shared her struggles, doubts about getting better, fears of not achieving her goals, and the prospects of her not being able to participate in her son's wedding. During these moments, I was ready to listen to her concerns and mindful to give her the space to say things out loud, without trying to give advice about fixing the situations. I am not a mental health specialist. The process of having regularly scheduled visits did set up a line of communication between us, but I worked hard to stay within my professional scope of practice.

A portion of my initial intake questionnaire asks my potential clients about their receiving support from a mental health specialist, therapist, or counselor. This helps to begin important conversations regarding mental health. If warranted, I will recommend a referral to a mental health specialist to make sure that my clients are receiving the best care—whole mind, body, and spirit care.

IT IS OKAY TO TAKE A BREAK

"Listening to your body" means paying attention to the subtle and often not-so-subtle messages that your body is communicating about your state of being. I often share with my clients that their personal therapeutic yoga practice is a daily commitment towards their long-term well-being. So, what happens when you get sick or don't feel well? This is when it is important to continue the process of listening to and honoring your body's needs by taking rest.

I have had clients report not feeling well, who worried that taking a few days off their programs to heal from a cold, flu, or other minor illness would undo all the progress that they had made in their therapeutic yoga practices. They reported beginning to feel the familiar tightness and restrictions that begin to return to their body when they skip a few days of their familiar routine.

I like to remind and reassure my clients that we will have days when our body needs time to rest so that it can heal from minor illness. Resting at the right time might just keep a minor illness from turning into a major challenge. This is an important part of the awareness practice that we take off the yoga mat and into our day to day living. This involves paying attention to your personal needs on all levels so that you know when to rest or make a change in your practice or other living skills when necessary. This is a form of awareness and flexibility that can go beyond the physical and often influences the mental and spiritual. This is a skill that can develop over time. With consistent practice we can continue working towards a state of balance in all things, as much as it is possible. We can learn how to find peace in the things that we cannot control, which in my experience is almost everything.

The feeling of extra tightness that we might feel when we have had a lapse in our practice often seems exaggerated because the body has gotten used to the sensation of the whole-body massage that has been occurring with a daily therapeutic yoga practice, which makes us feel pretty good. I have experienced similar challenges when I take the occasional break from my personal practices too. The good news is, we really have not lost our progress, the body remembers.

Allowing ourselves to have the time that we need to rest the body can be a great benefit to helping it heal more effectively. Yes, it may seem that we might have lost all the benefits that we gained because we often feel some of the familiar restrictions that had started to change over the months. This is temporary and will improve when we return gently to our regular program.

In this situation, I encourage my clients to not be too hard on themselves, to allow a gentle return to their practice, even if it means not holding a posture for as long or doing the stretches as far as they had done previously. Over time, their body will get back on track. When this happens, it is an opportunity for great learning. Things will never, ever be perfect. We can plan to keep on a schedule for the things that we want to accomplish, but life's adventures can get in the way. Our therapeutic yoga lifestyle practice that is set in mindfulness and paying attention, as well as having compassion for ourselves and others, can help us through these difficult times. I know that it has done wonders for me personally. Just another reason that I must share it.

CHAPTER 8

WEEK TEN: TEN WEEKS, A ROAD TRIP, AND SUCCESS

aroline greeted me at the door of her home. She was excited to tell me about an outing that she had with her husband over the weekend that required a two-hour drive, followed by a hike at a state park where they met for a family gathering and picnic. "I remembered what you said about sitting for long periods that could be related to my spine pain and the importance of taking standing breaks as often as possible. I wanted to make sure that I didn't have a problem with my back on this trip, so I made an extra effort to take breaks from sitting for a long time during the car ride. My husband and I stopped to get out of the car and stretch our legs about half-way to our destination."

I walked with Caroline towards the fitness room. "This is great news, Caroline. You're practicing your mindful awareness skills out in the world, and it seems like it was a great success."

Caroline stopped at the entrance to the fitness room, commenting, "We never did this during long car trips when the kids were young. It always seemed that we were in a rush to get to our destination. Times were different back then, there was so much going on. I gave all my attention to taking care of my family's needs, I didn't think much about what my needs were for a long time. I guess that might have contributed to my challenges. I'm working on this. I feel that I must make my self-care a priority if I want to keep my back pain from returning. The short driving breaks that we took on our recent trip made all the difference in the world. I feel like it helped me move better when we arrived. We had a great trip. I had no pain, and I was able to enjoy being active with my family. We did the same thing on our return trip back home."

Caroline moved into the fitness room and continued, "I've been eager for this session. I have something to show you." With that she walked over to a chair that she brought from her dining room, sat down, and removed her shoes and socks. Then she stood up and walked to her yoga mat. She began doing the Therapeutic Sun Salutation on her own. Breathing, bending, and squatting. Her execution was smooth, and her breathing gentle and coordinated with her movements. She adjusted her standing position to get her legs wider and was able to touch the floor on her own. She beamed.

She continued moving through the Therapeutic Sun Salutation© on the mat and then stepped back into downward-facing dog. She held the position for 10 breaths, strength showing in her arms, and she looked great. She transitioned down onto the floor. She held the quadruped position for five breaths, pressing the strength of her arms into the mat. She moved into cat/cow pose and kept her breath steady as she moved her spine alternately into extension and deep flexion. She demonstrated the thread the needle posture with ease and then moved into child's pose to stretch and take rest for five breaths.

When she rose back to her hands and knees, she transitioned to lying on her abdomen without a pillow for 10 breaths. Then up on to her elbows to hold the sphinx posture for 10 breaths. She rolled onto her spine with her knees bent and feet on the floor to show me her breathing activity practice, lengthening her exhalation and engaging her abdominals gently. I placed my index and middle finger along the edge of her abdomen near her rib cage and could feel the improvement in the activation of her abdominal muscles. She was stronger when I compared this to our first visit. This was a great sign.

She had been consistent and persistent in doing her homework. She had made significant progress in the last 10 weeks and her efforts were showing in an improved ability to move smoothly through the rest of the activities in her program. She completed the single-knee-to-chest stretch, then followed it with a gentle spine twist, moved into the hamstring stretch with strap, and followed that with the hip rotation activities and the supine figure-four [piriformis] stretch with strap.

MAKING PROGRESS TAKES EFFORT AND CONSISTENCY

Caroline moved on to do the therapeutic bridge pose and held the position with strong arms and legs for 10 breaths. She was able to keep her focus on maintaining smooth and rhythmic breathing during the activity. When she lowered her hips, she said, "The backs of my legs don't cramp up anymore. I remember the first time you asked me to do this, it was hard. I couldn't lift my hips."

I smiled, "You've improved not only the strength but also the endurance of your hamstring, gluteal, and extensor muscles along the backside of your body. Your progress shows itself in that the muscles can tolerate more effort. This is a great sign."

Caroline repeated the posture two more times, with small beads of perspiration beginning to form on her brow.

The therapeutic bridge pose is on my top 10 list of activities that I share with as many clients as possible. The therapeutic bridge pose is essential to developing strength and muscular endurance of the spine extensors and other muscles on the backside of the body to help make moving about and transitioning from lying down to getting up out of bed or off the floor more natural. Those activities are underappreciated because they are part of most people's day-to-day living activities. We don't realize how difficult that it can be to do these "basic" living activities until we have an injury or illness that influences our ability to function independently.

I could see the pride in her expression when I exclaimed, "Caroline, you've done a great job with your therapeutic yoga practice. I'm so encouraged. You were consistent and persistent in your efforts with your practices over these past 10 weeks. You worked with awareness, and you did all of this without bringing on a spasm. This is excellent."

Caroline rolled to her side and moved herself upright into sitting on her yoga mat with her legs stretched out ahead of her and responded, "I really focused my attention on maintaining my breathing in a gentle and smooth rhythm. It really soothed and calmed my mind. I've noticed that I've been using my focused breathing in other parts of my day when I'm feeling stressed. I use it when I'm out for my morning walks. It really helps me calm down. I never thought much about breathing before I started this therapeutic yoga practice, but this really works for me, and it feels good too."

I responded, "I'm happy that you recognize this tool. It has been within you your whole life. You're doing a great job accessing your SUPERPOWER."

Caroline chuckled and added, "Now all I need is a red cape, and I am good to go."

I smiled and added, "This would be a sight to see. Okay, now, you're nearing the end of your practice. Time to get your hips up on your cushions."

Caroline reached for the two flat cushions that she kept in the fitness room and proceeded to elevate her hips to position them under her body. She kept her breath calm throughout the action of getting into her supported position and gently lifted one leg and then the other until both legs were lengthened up to the ceiling. "I wasn't sure about this legs-up-the-wall thing when we first started doing it, but the more I do it, the more comfortable I'm getting. At this point, I find that I'm really enjoying it more than I imagined I could. It feels good. Sometimes, I do this at the end of a long day when I've been standing a lot."

Caroline settled into the supported legs-up-the-wall posture, brought her attention back to her gentle rhythmic breathing practice, and held the position for 10 breaths. I guided her in performing the basic foot and ankle activities. When she finished, Caroline bent her knees to return her feet to the mat, lifted her hips off the cushions, and moved into the resting (savasana) position. She rested for five minutes before I guided her back into the sitting position to complete the practice.

We reviewed the continuation of her home therapeutic yoga practice coupled with walking outdoors as weather permitted. Our session ended. Caroline walked me to her front door, and we said our goodbyes. I spent a few minutes making notes in my files before driving out to my next appointment for the day.

CHAPTER 9

WEEK TWELVE: THE BREATH AS YOUR GUIDE

A t the end of 12 weeks, Caroline was feeling better, and she was able to isolate and co-activate her abdominal muscles without moving any other part of her body. She was able to do this while keeping focused attention on maintaining smooth and rhythmic breathing. This takes a lot of focus, concentration, and effort. She demonstrated the results of her consistent effort over the long term.

Caroline shared, "I'm feeling stronger than ever. My grandkids came over last week, and I was able to get down on to the floor and play with them at their level. I took the opportunity to show them some of my stretches. I think they like that their grandma does yoga."

I congratulated Caroline on this important accomplishment.

She continued, "It was nice to be active with the grandkids. My back feels better than it has in a long time."

We moved into the fitness room to review her home therapeutic yoga practice and address any questions that she had. "Caroline, you've done extremely well taking charge of your therapeutic yoga practice. You've been doing the work, and now you're reaping the rewards. You don't need me anymore."

Caroline said, "I'm going to miss our time together, but I do feel confident that I can do this on my own. You helped me make my therapeutic yoga practice a regular part of my day. I'm on board. I never want to hurt again. I'm so happy to feel better because my son and future daughter-in-law are now in the process of planning their wedding, and I'm ready to help however I can."

It made me so happy to see the look of joy in Caroline's eyes when she spoke of her family. So often, we might hear about the benefits that our clients receive from participating in a therapeutic yoga program, but what many do not realize is that as practitioners, in any helping profession, we get the benefit of witnessing our clients' success. It is the BEST!

Caroline and I agreed to discontinue her private visits. She shared that she understood the importance and that she would continue with her regular program daily. I advised her that daily practice was essential, and that if she had a full week, at minimum, practicing three times per week would help her to maintain her progress, but that she should get back to a daily routine as soon as possible. "Caroline, your body is good at remembering what you have taught it. It won't forget over a long weekend, but you will likely feel a little less mobile when you take time off your program. Just get back into your practice and your body will return to balance."

Caroline shared, "I'm glad to hear this. I hadn't thought of stopping, but I guess something could get in the way of my practice. I'll try to remember this."

I responded, "Caroline, you have everything that you need within you to never have to go back to the state that you were in before we first met. You've experienced the benefits of participating in a breath-centered structured therapeutic yoga practice firsthand, and you've developed some great habits along the way over the past three months. I'm honored to have been able to help. I'm on your long-term wellness team, so if you need me, you know how to find me."

With that, we said our goodbyes. I left Caroline's home, happy to know that she had met all the goals that we had set on our first visit. She was independent in her therapeutic yoga program. She had improved her overall endurance and tolerance for walking daily, and was able to participate in all activities that brought her joy. She was empowered by her progress away from pain and content with her accomplishments over the last 12 weeks.

We checked in with each other every few months via email or with a phone call. Caroline's extreme debilitating back pain never returned. She implemented the practices into her daily life. Her program worked well for her. She knew exactly what to do and was able to take it with her when she traveled because she only needed a mat or a towel to lie on the floor. When she felt a little tweak in her body, she knew to listen carefully to her movements to help figure out what might be causing the challenge. She could use the breath-centered therapeutic yoga practice to mobilize her body. Her daily personal practice could help her recognize when she needed outside help from her doctor, physical therapist, or therapeutic yoga specialist.

We checked in with each other every few months over the next year to address a few questions. Eventually those calls stopped. Caroline was living a full life. She was pain-free, active, and happy to spend her time doing the things that she enjoyed with the people that she loved. I occasionally received a few postcards from her travels. Sweet success!

Practicing What I Preach

By this time, you have heard me extol the virtues of practicing breath-centered therapeutic yoga. I want to make it very clear that what I have shared with you in this book is not just me telling you to do something "because I said so." I do this practice. I have done variations of this practice over the years that I have been developing it. I know firsthand how it positively influences my whole body's spine and major joint mobility, how it helps to balance the muscle strength and stability of my feet, ankles, hips, knees, spine, shoulders, elbows, wrists, and hands. I know how the practice of paying attention to my body has helped me to recognize subtle changes that were beginning to happen in my posture or movements during my daily living activities that were beginning to create irritation, inflammation, and pain to my joints (arthritis).

I know how focusing my attention on maintaining smooth and rhythmic breathing during my personal fitness, cardiovascular, strength, and therapeutic yoga training activities has helped me to stay present. This helps me to recognize and avoid potential areas where I might be tempted to do more than my body is ready for or fall into repetitive stress situations. I also know that I have been successful in using focused attention on breathing to create a meditative state to relax, calm, and center my mind, and that it has had a beneficial influence on helping me down-regulate my overanxious nervous system over the years. Oh, yes, did I mention that I have suffered from symptoms of anxiety and mild depressive disorder over the course of my lifetime that I covered up with staying "busy" and being active? Oh, but that is a whole other book.

I do this practice because it works. I share this practice with others because I want them to know that they have options. We don't have to suffer. There Is much that we can do to reduce our functional limitations and improve our physical conditioning. I have provided a basic program of therapeutic yoga practices that I have shared with thousands of people over the years. I have personally experienced the benefits and have witnessed my clients improve their physical functioning over the long term. I know this works. If you don't believe me, give these activities a try. For the next three months, make time in your every day to do these practices. Take 30 minutes of your day to do it. If you only have 10 minutes, then do that. But do something. Keep your attention on your breath and experience the benefit of mobilizing every major joint in your body with care. Oh, yes, don't forget to check with your medical team to make sure that therapeutic yoga practices are right for you.

I hope that you will consider trying it.

CHAPTER **10**

NOTES FROM NYDIA

SMOOTH BREATHING MAKES A BIG DIFFERENCE

I have been asked many times why I emphasize the breathing activities so much. I have found that my clients demonstrate an improved response to participating in activities that are done with a focused attention on keeping the breath smooth throughout the whole process. I noticed this in my own self when I was developing these practices and began to share them slowly with my clients. It worked well, and I have continued to do so with every program that I have shared since.

I did not realize it when I first started focusing my attention on breathing in my personal practice, but it really was functioning as a form of meditation for me. I had read many books about yoga up to that time, and I am sure that those books probably spelled this out many times. I just don't recall seeing this spelled out directly. It is interesting that you can read about and study something, see it repeatedly, but in my case, I was not able to completely understand and integrate what I was reading until I had an embodied experience of it. I had to do the work and put the breathing activities into practice to recognize their true value. This philosophy continues to direct the way that I approach my personal wellness programs and those of my clients.

Caroline followed the instructions that I gave her regarding her breathing practices. She used the focused concentration on her breathing to calm her nervous system, invigorate her cells, warm up her body, and bring her attention to the present moment. She practiced this daily for three months, and this made the process second nature. It allowed her to recognize when she was doing more than her body was ready for during a therapeutic yoga posture or activity. It also helped her to know when she was working at the correct intensity. The benefits came in her ability to gradually increase the intensity and effort of her work while maintaining soft and rhythmic breathing. She was able to keep her mind calm during challenges that her body was experiencing. In my opinion, this is good practice. The skill of staying calm under pressure would benefit her in life skills and relationships that happened off her yoga mat. This can be true for the rest of us.

KEEP THE COMMUNICATION LINES OPEN WITH YOUR MEDICAL CARE TEAM. LET YOUR DOCTOR KNOW THAT YOU ARE INTERESTED IN PRACTICING THERAPEUTIC YOGA

You hear it at the beginning of a recorded video exercise session or read it at the beginning of this or other books that are sharing information about movement or exercise: "The information presented in this book or video is for educational purposes only and is not intended to substitute or to replace medical advice. Please consult with your physician to see if this or any other exercise program is right for you."

These recommendations are in this book and on so many programs that you might read or watch for very good reason. I will share with you why I think starting this conversation with your medical team is important, and it is not just to make my lawyer happy.

1. Having a good relationship with your physician and the team of humans that help you maintain and/or improve your health is important. This will set the groundwork for communicating your needs effectively and can make for a more pleasant long-term practitioner-patient relationship.
2. You should feel comfortable asking questions, no matter how trivial you might think that they might be, and you should feel that your physician is listening to your concerns.
3. Make a list of questions ahead of time when you are scheduled for a visit with your physician or other medical practitioner. This will help make sure that you don't forget anything that is important. We know that the time that we have for these appointments can be limited. Be prepared, and it can make a big difference for your long-term health.
4. You want to make sure that you follow the advice of your physician. Here is where effective communication is important. If you do not agree with the medical advice that your physician recommended, make sure to ask more questions

and have a conversation, instead of just ignoring the advice. Your optimal health and well-being can depend upon it.

5. If your medical team does not seem to be listening or communicating effectively, then if it is possible, consider changing your physician and/or health care team. You are a consumer of your health care. Making good choices in who provides your care can make a big impact in the relationship that you have with your medical team and can influence your long-term health and well-being.

6. Let your medical care team know that you are considering practicing therapeutic yoga. They may not be aware of the benefits that this mindful, breath-centered awareness practice can provide. This is an opportunity to educate your medical provider and get a sense of their experience or opinion with integrative therapeutic practices.

IMPROVING BALANCE REFERS TO MORE THAN NOT FALLING OVER

Important components of Caroline's program were working on bringing balance to her whole body by strengthening the backside of the body structures while lengthening the frontside of the body when necessary. Caroline continued the practice of lying on her stomach and gradually reduced the size of the small throw pillow to a folded bath towel. Eventually she was able to lie completely flat on her abdomen in comfort without any support. The process of a gradual introduction to extension of the lumbar and thoracic spine with support and then gradually reducing the amount of support over time was very important. Caroline was experiencing tightness in her hip flexors that was not normal, but unfortunately quite common for many individuals who suffer back pain and spasm. She was able to allow her body to slowly accommodate to the return of lumbar mobility while she was also developing strength of the gluteal and hip extensor muscles that would encourage balance in the hip joint and surrounding structures. This would go a long way into helping her have success in her long-term functional mobility goals.

She continued with the quadruped posture that would help to improve the connection between her shoulder girdle, rib cage, and torso. The cat/cow posture would improve her spine flexion and extension mobility. The downward-facing dog would improve mobility and stability to her spine and upper and lower body. The Therapeutic Sun Salutation© would continue to mobilize every major joint in her body, as well as improve her ability to transfer to the floor and get back up independently, a very important safety practice. Each posture in her program was implemented to meet *specific goals. Caroline was working toward the long-term goal of reconnecting with her body to gradually develop muscular endurance, core stability, and improved functional mobility. She was moving in the right direction.*

BEGIN BY DOING WHAT YOU CAN DO WITH SMOOTH AND RHYTHMIC BREATH AND PROGRESS SLOWLY. NO NEED TO RUSH. MORE IS JUST MORE, IT'S NOT ALWAYS BETTER

It is important to take your time to allow yourself to progress slowly when you are considering beginning a therapeutic yoga program or any type of physical activity. Take your time to explore the breathing activities. Do them daily. Really feel the sensation of movement in your body when you breathe. Once you have had some practice with your breathing activities in a supported position and in a place that makes it easy to focus, then begin to take your breathing awareness off the mat and into your daily activities. Notice how you breathe in different interactions with others and during your daily chores, work, or recreation.

Like most other exercise programs, the hardest part is getting started. Commit to performing your therapeutic yoga practice on a regular basis. Put it on your calendar to practice every day at a time that is realistic for you. Ten minutes is better than none. I find that once I get started, the physical practice feels so good that I want to do it for longer.

It is important to start at a level that is comfortable and does not cause you to strain, force, or push. This is where the breath comes in handy. If you can keep breathing smoothly while you are doing the practice, then you are working at the correct pace. You might have noticed that Caroline's program was not jam-packed with too many activities. That was on purpose. I prefer that my clients start with a few postures that they repeat regularly so that they can really connect their breathing to the practice. You can add postures into your program over time when you are comfortable.

Setting a solid foundation in the awareness of maintaining smooth and gentle breathing during your practice can help you know how much to do and can also help you recognize when your body is comfortable and ready for more. This helps you in the long term as you navigate through the therapeutic yoga practice that you will be able to continue on your own.

REPEAT THE PRACTICE, AGAIN AND AGAIN

The repetition in Caroline's practice was also very important. You may notice that we were building her program slowly over the weeks. After each session, Caroline was to put the latest postures and activities into her home therapeutic yoga practice. This allowed her body to get used to the activities that were designed to build her muscular endurance, overall mobility, strength, and flexibility. The repetition of her practice meant that she would perform each posture with awareness, and this could help us note her improvements over time. Her continued practice made it possible for Caroline to be able to feel her improvement.

Once her practice list got long, we would alternate activities throughout the week. We did this to keep her personal therapeutic yoga practice time within 30 to 45 minutes on most days.

The Western culture subscribes to the idea that "more is better," and I understand that there are times when this could be accurate. More well-being, more balance in life, and more world peace would be wonderful, but for the most part, more is just more, and it does not always mean that more is better.

Instead of spending more time in practice, make the effort to be consistent and persistent. This makes it possible to do "just enough" and to do it regularly. This is where we can see the benefits of our hard work.

DEVELOP A ROUTINE

Caroline was to perform her therapeutic yoga program daily when we were not meeting to develop a regular routine for her practice. She was instructed to be aware of her daily postural habits and positions, to avoid prolonged sitting, to have frequent standing stretch breaks, and to participate in daily walking outdoors or on a treadmill when needed.

Develop a regular routine for participation in the practices that you want to add to your life to make an impact for the better. Make the process easy to implement. Begin by looking at your day to determine times when you are most likely to succeed. You might find five minutes at the beginning of your day. You might notice that your afternoons have a consistent open time. You may notice that your day is full, but your evenings are more flexible. Just find a time that you can set a schedule to do your practice. Make it a regular thing.

Just like brushing your teeth, this is a part of overall health hygiene practice that can provide lifelong benefits when you do it on a regular basis. Yes, there will be times and situations in your life that may make it necessary to miss your program session, but do not let that discourage you. Come back to your regular routine as soon as possible. Your mind, body, and spirit will appreciate it.

DO THE WORK. NO ONE ELSE CAN DO THIS FOR YOU

This practice works. You've got to do it. No one can do it for you. You must incorporate it into your daily living, health, and hygiene practices, like brushing your teeth, sleeping, and eating. Long-term whole body and spine care is a process that involves paying attention. Be aware of things that could get you into trouble. One of the most common challenges is rushing through daily activities without awareness. Going into automatic mode and not paying attention to the subtle cues that your body is sending can be a recipe for disaster. Listen to your body. Take rest when you need it. Hydrate. Do the work. Every day. It is worth it. You can achieve high-quality functional living that lets you live free from debilitating pain.

You put in the effort every day. You do the work, so you can participate in the life that you want. In the process of living, we might occasionally feel a few aches and pains. I always say that the longer that we are on the planet, the higher the likelihood that we will experience change in our body, and some of it is not comfortable. I want everyone to know that we have the power within us to reduce our suffering. That means paying attention to and noticing the things that can increase our joint or muscle pain. That includes keeping our mental health as a priority. Stress contributes to many of our challenges when we are living with pain. Keeping active, hydrating well, eating foods that honor our health and reduce inflammation, getting enough good sleep, taking time to be outdoors, paying attention, keeping our minds balanced, fostering relationships, and being in community with others can go a long way towards improving our long-term quality of life and our physical and mental functioning.

CONSISTENT EFFORT CAN PROVIDE SIGNIFICANT RESULTS

Here is the thing. Our culture wants everything to come prepackaged and ready to go. To be put in pill form for ease and convenience. We are sedentary when compared to our ancestors, with the advent of the Industrial Age and commercialization of food sourcing. We don't hunt for food, grow our crops, sew our own clothes, wash our clothes in a washtub, or walk to the well or river for water. We are surrounded by convenience, which makes it less necessary for us to move. In the name of progress, we are losing a prized gift: our mobility, strength, muscular endurance, and well-being. Our bodies were designed to move. Every cell, muscle, organ, and structure in our body is benefited by the motion that invigorates them, that pulls and pushes on them. The fascia that connects every tissue, bone, and muscle.

It really does start with the breath. The connective tissue that surrounds the diaphragm is woven into and influences the cardiac sac that surrounds and protects the heart. The movement of breathing influences and massages the internal organs. Breathing influences the subtle movement of the rib cage as it connects to the thoracic spine. The thoracic spine connects to and influences the cervical spine above it and the lumbar spine below it. The thoracic spine also connects the rib cage to the collarbone in a small joint space that lies at the base of the front of the neck that then connects to the shoulder blade, the upper arm, forearm, wrist, and hand. The cervical spine influences and connects to the skull, and the lumbar spine influences and connects to the sacrum and pelvis, which connect to the thigh bones, knees, lower legs, ankles, and feet. There is no accident in our creation.

SAVASANA—A SANSKRIT WORD FOR THE RESTING POSTURE— AKA "CORPSE POSE"

When I was reading and studying about yoga in books, I regularly saw the term "corpse pose" used for the end-of-practice resting posture that, in Sanskrit, is called "savasana." I seldom use the term "corpse pose" for the resting posture when I lead therapeutic yoga practices. Sometimes I choose to use the Sanskrit word "savasana," but most often, I just instruct my clients to "take rest" at the end of the physical practice. I am not a Sanskrit scholar, so I lean towards using the English translations when referring to the therapeutic yoga postures and the variations that I share with my clients. About the English translation "corpse pose," I will be honest and share that I was initially surprised by it, but it began to make sense to me when, over the years, I read the descriptions and definitions of the term as explained by various authors, especially when I began to become more proficient in its practice.

Yogapedia.com defines savasana and shares that it is the Sanskrit name for an important restorative posture that is commonly used at the end of a sequence of yoga postures for the purpose of relaxation and integration. The site also shares that since the entire length of the body is connected to the earth when in the pose, the practice of savasana can be deeply grounding and may cultivate the inner stillness and stability necessary for personal growth. I agree with these statements. I believe that savasana is an important component of the movement practices and should not be missed.

BUT WHAT ABOUT THE FACT THAT THE DOCTORS TOLD CAROLINE THAT SHE HAD A BULGING DISC AND BONE SPURS?

In our initial interview, Caroline reported and shared documentation of having had a history of a slight disc bulge and changes in the bone structure along her lumbar spine. I always appreciate having this information because it helps to create a clearer picture of my client and informs the development of their therapeutic yoga program. Despite what many might believe, her having this medical history did not automatically make her a candidate for physical therapy services. In this situation, the direction of Caroline's program was determined by other factors and related to the fact that she was not experiencing active symptoms of pain or spasm when we met for our sessions.

The presence of active pain and spasm and other factors are what help me to identify the best method to serve a potential patient/client.

There have been a few instances where the result of a consultation determined that the client would be better served by a referral to a specific medical specialist or a yoga or other fitness professional that I believed would be most effective in helping to address and meet the client's goals.

Having the most complete medical history possible is important to my being able to support a client most effectively in their physical therapy and/or therapeutic yoga programing. Caroline's history of changes in her spine, with occasional episodes of back pain and spasm, has been familiar to me over the years. I have devoted a significant portion of my professional career to help others move past spine, neurologic, orthopedic, or other problems that limit their function and quality of living. In Caroline's case, these findings were discovered and diagnosed several years before our sessions started and were part of her medical imaging history. Despite the presence of these structural changes, it wasn't clear that they were the source of her pain and spasm.

This is a familiar pattern. I had seen many clients in my physical therapy and therapeutic yoga consultation practices that presented with similar changes in their spine. These people had experienced occasional events of back pain and dysfunction and responded well to physical therapy and therapeutic yoga interventions and were subsequently able to move forward and live a full life with the ability to mitigate or eliminate pain and spasm, and yet they still had the bony and disc changes.

According to the Mayo Clinic, bone spurs (osteophytes) can occur where bones meet at joints and can form on the bones of the spine. The main cause is traced to osteoarthritis (inflammation of the bone and joints). Bone spurs are not always associated with pain, as many people who are living with bone spurs also report no pain. Most people do not even realize that they have bone spurs until an X-ray or MRI shows them. There is not a conclusive cause and effect when someone has bone spurs that they will also have pain. There are so many other factors to consider when a person is living with pain. There are some situations where bone spurs cause loss of motion in the joints and pain.

An example in the spine: Bone spur formation can narrow the space where the spinal cord travels through in your spinal column. Bone spurs can narrow the space where the spine nerve root exits from the spinal column. This situation can create pressure on the spinal cord or nerve root and can cause pain. If the bone pressure is the cause of the problem, then some patients will benefit from surgical intervention to create more space. The cause of pressure to the spinal nerves is not always the actual bone pressing on the spinal nerve root. Most often it is the pressure in the joint space that is created by the inflammation that is in the joint when the body is trying to heal the bony changes that are happening in the joint. That explains why the most common form of treatment for patients living with bone spurs who have pain is anti-inflammatory medication. Surgery is not the first line of treatment.

Some of the most effective solutions that help persons to reduce pain caused by inflammation involve incorporating stress-reducing lifestyle and dietary changes into long-term daily living practices. Caroline's mindful, breath-centered awareness therapeutic yoga practices helped her back in the days before our mainstream culture realized the importance of reducing inflammation for long-term health. She was ahead in the game.

BULGING DISCS IN THE SPINE?

The interesting thing about spine health and back pain is that there has been no conclusive relationship made between bulging discs and back pain. It is quite common for persons to present with significant disc bulges or herniations in their spine and not have any pain. At the same time, it is also common for persons to have significant debilitating pain and spasm, and not present with any signs of disc or bony changes in the spine.

MRI diagnostics have improved our understanding of what is happening inside of a person's body. Over the years, spine imaging led to improvements in understanding the physiological changes that might be the cause of pain. Early in the use of this technology, it was generally understood that a bulge or change in the spine physiology was evidence of the source of pain, and this made surgical correction popular.

In the '90s, having an MRI that showed such changes would have automatically meant that spinal surgery would be recommended and/or performed to change the situation. We are fortunate that we now understand a lot more about the way the spine and the nervous system work. Ongoing research has demonstrated that back pain may not be happening as a direct result of a disc herniation. Studies suggest that imaging findings of degenerative spine changes are generally part of the normal aging process and not always indicative of pathologic changes that require surgical or other intervention. Such studies have also noted that even among patients with back pain, the degenerative findings on MRIs are not always associated with the degree or presence of low back pain and that it is important to take this into consideration when interpreting the significance of the imaging findings. The imaging findings must be interpreted in the context of the patient's clinical condition.

There are many other factors to consider when we attempt to understand the source of pain that might be affecting a person, and those factors have been found to influence people in many ways. It is important for me to share that there is much to consider when trying to understand the complexity of pain and that this goes way beyond the scope of the information that I will be presenting here.

I can share that ongoing research has begun to identify the role that the nervous system plays in people who are living with pain. I am referring to the parts of the nervous system that are automatically processing information that we might not always be aware of.

(See autonomic nervous system in Chapter 4.) These findings are making the connection between stress, trauma, and the biological, psychological, and social factors that are influenced by the human condition that can impact the nervous system and create or keep a person living with pain. I won't expand upon this topic here. I encourage those of you who want to learn more about this to look at the reference section at the end of this book for some resources that can help you to begin to make sense of the complex nature of pain. The good news is that we are getting better at understanding it every day.

As always, I recommend that my clients get as much information as they can about their situation, work towards assembling an excellent team to support their situation, and ask many questions along the way. I will be sharing more about this idea of learning as much as you can about your situation or condition in the sections to come.

LEARN AS MUCH AS YOU CAN ABOUT HOW YOUR BODY FUNCTIONS

Our body is an amazing structure that has systems that are intricately connected and integrated together to serve a purpose on this planet. Each part of us is influenced by the other parts even though they may not seem related. There are systems within the intricate inner workings that we don't even know are functioning that influence our daily living. Many of these systems depend on movement to help the body function optimally. I like to encourage my clients to help their body parts move as they were intended. To feed them well, hydrate them well, work them efficiently. and move them regularly. To train them to tolerate increased loads and stress under pressure while maintaining calm and to make sure to rest them well on a regular basis to keep the whole system running efficiently for a lifetime.

ALWAYS CONSIDER THE SOURCE OF THE INFORMATION THAT YOU ARE GETTING ABOUT YOUR CONDITION

I am not a surgeon, and I don't do surgery. I always inform my clients that they should consider the source of the information that they are getting. Since I do not provide a surgical option, it might seem unlikely that I would be recommending surgery. This is not true. During the time that I am working with my clients, if there is something that shows up during their initial therapeutic yoga assessment or physical therapy evaluation that warrants medical attention, I will refer the client back to their primary care provider or encourage them to seek a consultation with a specialist as it is needed. If something changes in their condition over the time that I am working with a client, I share my observations and advise them to communicate with their primary physician or medical team.

Over the years, I have created a network of medical specialists that I refer my clients to and who also refer clients back to me. I have a list of excellent surgeons in a variety of specialties that I often refer my clients to when they present with conditions that warrant the opinion and assessment of a surgical consultation. This list includes medical specialists that I have met over the course of the years, some of whom have sought me out specifically because they have become aware of the specialized work that I do helping my clients return to function with therapeutic yoga. Others are specialists that learned about my services from their patients. My clients' optimum health and safety are my primary concern.

I am grateful to these specialists who utilize an integrative approach in the care of their patients. We certainly need more of these amazing beings. The next time that you go in for a check-up, ask your medical team what they think about using therapeutic yoga to address spine health. If they don't have an opinion, share this book with them.

WHEN EVERY OTHER OPTION HAS FAILED: THE LAST RESORT

There are many instances when my clients come to me as a "last resort" before moving forward with heavy pharmaceutical or surgical treatment options. These clients are typically referred to me by their pain doctors, orthopedists, neurologists, osteopaths, chiropractors, primary care specialists, psychologists, counselors, and even other physical therapists. They are often motivated by the seriousness of the pharmaceutical treatment or surgical procedure that has been recommended, and they, along with their medical practitioner, want to make certain that they have experienced and exhausted every conservative approach before moving forward. I am always grateful for the opportunity to work with clients in this situation, which is already incredibly stressful and overwhelming to them. The process of the consultation that I provide is like my therapeutic yoga assessment and physical therapy evaluation, somewhat of a hybrid of these two where we will determine together what tools will be best to use to empower the client.

For those whose condition will be most effectively approached by surgical intervention, I offer a program to prepare the client for surgery. This involves education on using diaphragmatic breathing and mindfulness to reduce stress, as well as gentle strengthening and lengthening of muscles and joint structures that might be influenced by the surgical intervention. We will brainstorm methods for completing necessary functional daily living tasks after the surgery, like transferring safely out of bed, to the toilet, and even how to get off the floor in case of a fall. These are all things that were part of a physical rehabilitation program that had been traditionally taught to patients after a surgery when they spent a week, and sometimes even a month in a rehabilitation hospital. This was in the past. These days, most people who have a spine surgery or joint replacement might spend a night or two in the hospital. Others experience day surgery and are sent home for their recovery. There is often a gap in the time that they receive home health and/or outpatient physical therapy. My goal is to educate my client to give them the tools that they will need and develop a program that they can use to get their body moving and breathing with awareness to make the transition back to balance and healing more effective.

There are other things that I share with my clients who are preparing for a surgery, and the topics revolve around each client's specific needs. One of the most important things that I share is that I want them to remember to begin their gentle diaphragmatic breathing as soon as they open their eyes after surgery. This will help improve their oxygenation, help to encourage their relaxation response, and help to rid their body of the influence of the anesthesia more effectively. This can also help speed the healing response and help them return to normal function.

GUT HEALTH MATTERS

Many of my clients are not aware of the importance and influence of their gut health and motility when they are in hospital recovering after a surgery. One of the important things that will help you get out of a hospital sooner and helps to reduce complications is the proper functioning of the gastrointestinal system. If you are fortunate to not have had many surgeries or hospital stays, you may not be aware that anesthesia, necessary medications (including pain medication), and the stress of surgery can have an impact on the gut's natural function. Part of the process for determining a patient's level of readiness for discharge from the hospital can be influenced by whether they are able to successfully pass urine, have had a bowel movement, and/or are passing gas.

I teach my clients about the impact that pain medications have on slowing down the gut and possibly causing constipation, and why it is important for them to move their body and walk as soon as possible (when it is safe and medically appropriate) because that stimulates the gastrointestinal system to work, helping to pass gas and to have a bowel movement. Yes, their hospital stay length could be influenced by pooping and peeing. Talk about stress.

I would like to add that the use of appropriate prescribed pain medication is very important in the early days directly following a surgical procedure. This can help make the patient more comfortable and that can encourage their ability to move in the early stages of post-surgical activities. It is not within my scope of practice to give advice or recommendations on dose or type, that is where the open communication between the patient and their entire healthcare team plays an important role in the success of their recovery.

CLIENTS WHO ARE SEEKING AN OPINION REGARDING DELAYING OR AVOIDING SURGERY

When an individual is seeking my opinion regarding their potential for having, delaying, or avoiding a surgery altogether, I will ask them the following questions:

1. *Are you in constant pain, or does it change throughout the day?*
2. *What treatment approaches have you tried? Physical therapy, osteopathic, chiropractic, acupuncture, massage?*
3. *Are you currently active in regular cardiovascular and endurance exercise like walking, swimming, running, dancing, or cycling?*
4. *Does your pain or motion limitation interfere with your ability to accomplish your essential daily living tasks like grooming, feeding, sleeping?*
5. *Does your condition/situation interfere with your ability to make a living?*
6. *Are you responsible for others?*
7. *Is your situation negatively impacting your quality of life?*
8. *Are you aware of the risks that come with any surgical intervention?*
9. *Are you willing to do the work with your surgical team by following up with recommended rehabilitation and therapies to support the best possible outcome after the surgical intervention?*

10. *Are you aware that there is still work to be done post-surgical intervention to bring you back to full functioning, and are you willing to do it?*
11. *Will you have the support of a caregiver during this process to drive you to appointments, help you at home upon discharge, and help you to take care of essential needs directly after the surgical intervention?*

I ask these questions to encourage a conversation with the client and to make sure that they are realistic in their expectations of what the surgical intervention can provide. I am not against surgery. I want the client to understand that a surgical intervention is not always the "quick fix" that they might be hoping for, that there is very important work to be done after the surgery that has the potential to help them achieve the desired result. I want them to be fully aware of those things.

I also want to encourage the idea of preparing for a surgical intervention, or as I like to call it, "being in training for an upcoming surgery." In the early days of the physical therapy work that I did in the '90s, the concept of "pre-habilitation," otherwise known as doing preparatory rehabilitation activities to prepare for a surgery, was common. This happened in the time when the insurance and third-party payer system recognized the cost effectiveness of such programs for the patient's best outcome. It is unfortunate that this process quickly became out of favor with third-party payers who (in my opinion) may have decided to cut costs. I am hopeful that this will change.

LEARN AS MUCH AS YOU CAN ABOUT YOUR SITUATION OR CONDITION

I believe that knowledge is power. I teach my clients as much as they care to learn about how their physical body works, the structure of the spine, the muscles, bones, connective tissue, nervous system, and any other systems that may be influenced by their situation. We work on increasing their awareness of postural habits that may be encouraging challenges to their daily living and methods to implement new habits that can make a change for the better.

When I provide private physical therapy care, it is essential that I provide a thorough evaluation of the patient's condition so that I can begin to identify the source of the problem that might be causing their acute symptoms. I approach my therapeutic yoga clients similarly, even though they don't have acute symptoms of an injury or problem. They often come to me for help with a chronic situation or to help them return to an improved level of functioning. In some cases, they come to me to help prevent problems in the future.

I prefer to keep a positive and realistic attitude when I am addressing the challenges that my clients are facing, whether in physical therapy or therapeutic yoga work. I try to help them become more aware of the wonderful ways that their bodies, minds, and spirits work together, even when some of their systems are not cooperating. I have also found that my clients respond more effectively when I then share how some of the residual effects of healing after an injury or surgery (like swelling that can cause pain) are signals that the body is just doing its best to help and heal itself. This often helps my clients to stop feeling like their body is working against them. With this approach and some continued learning about their condition, I find that my clients begin to understand the mechanisms behind the problem that might have put them in the situation that brought them to me in the first place.

I also like to make sure that my clients understand that the source of their challenges might need the support of professionals outside the scope of the therapeutic yoga practice. When appropriate, I refer my clients to seek the support of a myriad of specialists in mental health, osteopathic, chiropractic, massage therapy, specialized physical therapy, or integrative medicine. Many of the goals that we create together are centered around improving functional living skills that are directed towards improving quality of living for the long term of their whole selves. I share with my clients that we are not working towards perfection, but rather an awareness of an improved state of being. It is wonderful to witness the transformation in their thinking about their situation from irritation and despair to one of hope and possibility. I just LOVE this job.

SAFETY, THE NERVOUS SYSTEM, AND THE NATURE OF PAIN

Over the years, I have had the opportunity to have many conversations with my clients about the state of "being in pain" that they were experiencing. Many of them came to me as a last resort and often they came with stories about friends, family members, and even medical practitioners who they thought were exhausted hearing about their pain that seemed to have no sign of reduction or relief. They often shared a similar belief that others seemed to think that they were making it up or that it was all in their head.

I have thoughts about this statement, "The pain is all in your head." I have heard this phrase made as a direct statement or asked in the form of a question many times. When a client takes the time to explain this to me and when they ask me my opinion, I share my thoughts with them carefully. I often share that I think that there could be something behind this idea of pain being all in our head, since I have come to understand (by following the science on the subject) that the experience of pain exists within the nervous system. Since the brain, the command center of the nervous system, lies in the skull, well, maybe there is something to the saying that pain is all in our head, or at least its origin is within the nervous system. I think more people need to understand this idea for what it is.

When I share this idea, I often get a strange look from my client until I expand on the idea by sharing about the autonomic nervous system and my understanding of the vagus nerve (the tenth cranial nerve) and its seemingly complex myriad of influence within the body's systems. At first glance, it can seem complex, but once you read it over a hundred times, it begins to make sense. ☺

Dr. Stephen Porges said it best in the foreword that he wrote for Stanley Rosenberg's book, Accessing the Healing Power of the Vagus Nerve. In the foreword, Porges shared his own personal story of suffering back pain and seeking a consultation with Stanley Rosenberg who then proceeded to gently move the tissues in Porges's body that signaled it to relax. Porges is the scientist that developed the polyvagal theory, which has provided new insights into the way our autonomic nervous system unconsciously mediates social engagement, trust, and intimacy.

In his writing, Porges states:

> I understood immediately what [Stanley Rosenberg] was doing. The physical manipulation, gently moved the upper levels of tissue, signaled the body to relax. The relaxation was sufficient to reorganize the neural muscular regulation that supported the spine, allowing the vertebra to gently fall into place. Thus Stanley was transmitting signals of safety to the neuromuscular system that enabled the system to immediately shift from a defensive state of contraction, in which it attempted to protect the vulnerability of the lower spine, to a state of safety in which a gentle touch would functionally allow the system to find its natural position.

Here Porges was saying that the gentle movements that Stanley Rosenberg had him experience allowed the body to relax enough so that the spine could move closer to its balanced position. The experience transmitted a state of "being safe" within the nerve and muscle system, which allowed it to stop fighting (holding tension) in order to protect itself. This led to a state of comfort that allowed a very gentle touch to move it into or closer to balance. That state of "being in balance" then caused the emergency state of "being in pain" to no longer be needed. This then allowed him to be able to move more effectively without pain. The body trusted itself, so it could return to more natural movement.

This process that Porges described pretty much explains the science behind why the Therapeutic Astanga Method© and similar therapeutic practices that provide a meditative, focused concentration on the melding of the breath, mind, and gentle movements work. I have been taking my experience of working with the nervous system in the rehabilitation of physical therapy patients with spinal cord injuries, strokes, head injuries, and peripheral nerve injuries over the last few decades, and combining it with the traditional yogic lifestyle principles that I was studying and implementing into my own personal practices along with the principles that I followed within traditional fitness and exercise to create methods that help people use the tools that they have within themselves to improve their ability to function.

This is how the Therapeutic Astanga Method© emerged over the course of a few decades. TAM© is all about the nervous system and the processes that we can use to down-regulate it—to calm it down when it is in a state of emergency or panic. The gentle movement awareness practices use the breath as a focal point to create a form of movement meditation, which serves to relax the nervous system to create a sense of ease and comfort. This process works to reduce the defense mechanisms within the nervous system that could keep a person in spasm and pain. With the defenses down, muscles, nerves, bones, and fascia can now have an opportunity to reorganize and accept new patterns of movement that can lead a person towards living their best functional life.

BAREFOOT PRACTICE IS BEST

Over the years, I have been asked by my students if it is necessary to do their yoga practice in bare feet. I suspect that this question arose for some who might be shy about the appearance of their feet. My response to this question has not changed much over the years. I recommend the practice be in bare feet, no socks, or shoes, although socks are encouraged if the temperature in the room is cool, but I believe that it is best to remove socks when practicing standing postures. There are several reasons that I give for this recommendation.

1. When an individual takes time to practice in bare feet, they also get an opportunity to inspect the skin color, temperature, and condition of the toes and feet. The feet and toes are the furthest from your brain and your heart. When there is a slight change in the cardiovascular or the nervous system, the feet can be one of the first places that reflects these subtle changes. You can get a lot of information about the state of health in your body when you regularly inspect your toes and feet.
2. Many individuals are not aware of the habitual pattern of positioning of their feet in standing. They may not notice habits of weight bearing on the outside of the feet, collapsing arches, foot muscle atrophy, or recognize that the callous formation, corns, or hammer toes are not necessarily inherited in their genetic code, but typically occur because of poor-fitting, sized-too-small shoes.
3. Practicing standing postures in bare feet allows the muscles in the lower leg and foot to have the opportunity to do what they were intended to do without being restricted by shoes.
4. Practicing while wearing socks can influence the positioning of the toes and limit their ability to stretch out naturally to make the best contact on the mat when in standing activities.
5. Practicing in bare feet allows for grounding connection to the earth. This practice can be relaxing to the nervous system.
6. Practicing in bare feet can be the beginning of a person's journey towards improved awareness of the importance of setting a solid foundation that begins from the ground up. The foot structure and position on the mat (when optimally aligned) can then positively influence the knee, hip, pelvis, spine, etc. When there is a collapse in the arch of the feet, this breakdown can negatively influence the knees, hips, etc. Many joint and arthritic challenges can be reduced when a person begins to work on improving the position and alignment in the feet.
7. Awareness of improving the strength, flexibility, and mobility of the foot and ankle structures and their position in space can help reduce arthritic changes to other joints in the body by helping the body maintain a healthy "spring" in the foundation that can influence a balanced alignment in other joints.

8. *Foot exercises that focus on developing the strength and mobility of the important muscles that influence the foot and ankle become awareness practices that can reduce the risk of falls and that can potentially have a positive influence on a person's long-term function and wellbeing.*

Many of my clients experience the beginning of their therapeutic yoga practices with minimal standing activities and more supported lying postures. Having the feet bare and giving specific cues for keeping an awareness of their feet is still important. This helps to keep the individual working with their whole body in mind and prepares them for progressing their practice in the future. Yes, this is all about setting a solid foundation for a lifetime of well-being.

BEING ABLE TO GET DOWN ONTO THE FLOOR AND THEN BACK UP—IT COULD SAVE YOUR LIFE

I have spent the last few decades focusing my efforts towards sharing the therapeutic yoga practices that I have been developing with as many people as possible. Working with elders—or the "Wisdom Warriors," as I prefer to call them, has been most rewarding. I have learned so much from these amazing beings.

One of the challenges that I notice my elder clients facing as they grow older, is the fear of falling and fracturing a hip. I've noticed this in elders of all backgrounds. If you get a group of elders talking, it is inevitable that one will bring up a story of someone that they know who has fallen and a medical problem resulted, or they died due to the fall.

As a young physical therapist, I understood that falls were one of the leading complications that could lead to severe injury and/or death in the elder population. I was trained to help my patients to learn how to get up off the floor and, in some cases, even to teach them to fall more effectively to reduce the risk of head trauma and fractures.

These experiences have influenced the way that I approached program development for my physical therapy patients and that also had a significant impact on the way that I approached the clients and students that I worked with in my therapeutic yoga practices, especially with the large numbers of persons who attended group therapeutic yoga classes at my studio. In 10 years, over 10 thousand new students came through the doors, and because we practiced primarily on the floor, that meant that each person was going to get some experience trying to move down to and up off the floor. That is not to say that I didn't offer alternatives. We had some students who participated in therapeutic yoga practices in chairs, wheelchairs, with assistive devices, prosthetics, etc., but they all had to eventually practice getting down onto the floor and then back up with help. It was important. It was a safety thing.

The most effective method that I use to get people safely down to the floor and then back up is the Therapeutic Sun Salutation© that I developed over the course of 27 years.

I like to make sure that every person that I work with can move down to the floor and then get up off the floor with as much grace as possible. I don't discriminate when it comes to this. I teach everyone—young and old, fit or frail. Everyone that I encounter gets their own version of this important practice.

I teach this to as many people as I can. I have been fortunate to share this with the yoga teachers that I have trained. At my state's physical therapy conferences I have presented this approach to physical therapists, assistants, educators, and students. I share the Therapeutic Sun Salutation© because it gently mobilizes every major joint of the body, gives the practitioner information about how well their body moves, helps to identify any limitations that need improvement, and because it is a method that prepares the body to have the mobility and strength that will make getting down to and then up off the floor easier. "Easy" is in the body of the beholder when it comes to getting off the floor. This does take practice and consistent effort.

At the end of the day, it all comes down to safety. I believe that it is a major problem if you end up on the floor and you can't get back up. It doesn't matter whether you do it on your own, with help, or use the support of a chair or other piece of furniture. Being able to get up off the floor can save your life. Not being able to get up off the floor can lead to an unplanned early exit from the planet and can be avoided with proper training and practice. There, I said it. Now, get to practicing.

WHY THERAPEUTIC YOGA RESEARCH?

"This practice works … I know that it has benefits because I have done the research." This is a phrase that I have enjoyed sharing with my therapeutic yoga clients and students over the past 14 years.

Since 2009 I have been collaborating with the University of Texas Health System in San Antonio, Texas, to create therapeutic yoga intervention programs for yoga and cancer research. In that time, our research has established, in randomized controlled trials, that the therapeutic yoga intervention is equally effective as traditional exercise and improves the well-being of survivors of breast cancer. The research program that we delivered to survivors of cancer in 2020 also concluded that therapeutic yoga delivered via livestream showed improvement in respiratory capacity, improvements in a timed walk test, and showed significant reduction in inflammatory cytokines that were circulating in the blood of our participants. These participants practiced the intervention three times per week for four months.

Some of the benefits that our team has identified as a result of our research have been documented in published manuscripts.

The survivors of cancer who participated in therapeutic yoga three times per week for four to six months were found to have experienced the following:

- Improvements in their breathing function
- Reduction in the number of cells in the immune system that stimulate inflammation
- Improvements in their functional mobility, flexibility, and strength
- Improvements in the distance that they can walk when measured using the six-minute timed walk test

I should add too that in the research, we found that therapeutic yoga presented via livestream demonstrated similar benefits to in-person presentations.

Therapeutic yoga was found to be as effective as other traditional forms of exercise, such as strength and cardiovascular training, to benefit survivors of cancer.

This study was impacted by the Covid-19 pandemic. To meet the safety and health needs of the study participants and therapeutic yoga instructors, our team decided to stop the live, on-site therapeutic yoga classes. I had started to livestream my therapeutic yoga classes for the Nydia's Yoga Therapy studio small-group classes and the Open Hand Institute Therapeutic Yoga teacher training program and recommended that we change the protocol to allow livestream instead of in-person classes. It was important to improve overall safety for all and to continue with the study that we had prepared for in the two years leading up to the pandemic. It worked. We were able to continue the study and keep the participants actively engaged during a challenging time within our communities.

Looking back at it now, it is hard to believe that the practice that I developed and was doing for my own personal long-term well-being in my living room could evolve into practices that I would share with the community of people who were interested in long-term hea th in San Antonio and also lead to working with a cancer research team.

I opened Nydia's Yoga Therapy studio against strong odds of success as a self-directed entrepreneur. I felt that the brick-and-mortar location would give me a respectable platform that (at the time) I felt that I needed to be taken seriously within the medical community. This was in the early 2000s. My own insecurities about not fitting into the mold of the traditional clinic set up to offer my services were rising and fed the idea. Up until that time, I had been sub-leasing space in karate studios, fitness gyms, schools, and community centers, and working in my clients' homes. I was amazed that physicians were referring my services to their patients who then had to track me down in order to access my private and small group therapeutic yoga programs and consultations. I really wanted to establish myself as a leader in the industry for therapeutic yoga, locally and possibly globally. Yes, I am a woman with big dreams. I went through great expense and incredible stress to make the work that I had been doing that was considered "outside of the box" more legitimate by opening a studio in a commercial location to make it easier for me to share the integrative practices that I had developed with the medical, yoga, and fitness communities in the area.

I share this because the commercial location opened the doors for the therapeutic yoga and cancer research that I continue to do with our team. The research helped us to report the benefits that I shared earlier. Dr. Amelie Ramirez—director of the Institute for Health Promotion Research (IHPR), chair of the Department of Population Health Sciences, Associate Director of Cancer Outreach and Engagement at the Mays Cancer Center at UT Health San Antonio, and contributor to this book, generously authoring its foreword—has been a longtime advocate and practitioner of health and wellness over the years and was a participant in my group fitness classes in the early '90s. She stopped at my studio when she recognized my name and quickly became a member. It was her idea to start doing the research. I am forever grateful for the opportunity to expand my offerings to a wider audience and to contribute to the development of programs that will help survivors of cancer improve their quality of life for the long term. Who you meet can change your life. Dr. Amelie Ramirez changed mine for the better.

Interestingly enough, within a year of opening the commercial location, I began to yearn for the setup that I have now. I wanted to have a studio on my home property with a few acres of land to garden, grow vegetables, raise chickens, and create a peaceful environment for my clients, myself, and my family. I felt that this environment could help me practice what I preach while I expanded the work that I love in doing therapeutic yoga research, writing, leading small group therapeutic yoga classes, offering private consultations, and promoting therapeutic yoga in speaking engagements worldwide. Now I have what I feel is the best environment for me to continue offering my services to the local and global community.

I am happy to announce that our research team is continuing to produce and publish manuscripts and working on future projects utilizing the therapeutic yoga intervention that I have continued to develop, supervise, monitor, and implement.

A BOOK CAN BE A GREAT WAY TO GET STARTED

Ideally, therapeutic yoga would be delivered individually, in person, with direct instruction and supervision from an experienced therapeutic yoga specialist. This was Caroline's experience because she met the right person, at the right time; she acted on advice, she made the call, she learned new skills, did the work, and it gave her the opportunity to change her life for the better.

If this work is best delivered in person, what makes me think that there could be any benefit to sharing it in book form?

I started to learn about yoga by reading books. It makes sense to me that I should give the opportunity to others who, like me, might read or listen to this book and get something started.

I knew that I had to write this book to share the method that I had developed that combined a unique approach to my experiences in physical therapy, fitness, and yoga. I do these practices. I have done the research and I know that there is great value and that there are significant health benefits to implementing a therapeutic yoga practice into our daily lives.

The reality is that not everyone has the time, resources, or the desire to make that type of commitment to something that they know very little or nothing about. Think about it. Did you know anything about therapeutic yoga before you picked up this book? Caroline knew nothing about therapeutic yoga but decided to take a chance, to make a call acting on the advice of a person that she had just met to see if she could do something to help herself and finally find a way to reduce the pain that she was experiencing that seemed to be getting worse with each passing year.

There are still very few physical therapists who are practicing "outside of the traditional box" within the integrative world of therapeutic yoga. But the good news is that the list is growing. Many of my clinical peers are expanding their personal and professional education in techniques that involve a more comprehensive approach to their patients and it is benefiting them just as much as their patients. The number of Yoga Therapists (certified yoga teachers who have expanded their education and subsequently have received at minimum 800 hours of specific training in yoga therapy with mentorships and continuing study post certificate) is growing—see IAYT.org for more information. I hold a certificate as a yoga therapist, grandfathered through the certification process after an extensive application process to determine my experience in the practices that would meet their stringent requirements for certification. I share this because it might help you find a practitioner that you can add to your long-term health awareness program.

I wrote this book not so much as a substitute for individualized instruction but as a gateway to a method that might help persons on the path to wholeness. I knew that there are people who might never have the chance to come to one of my therapeutic yoga classes live or online, but they might find out about this book. I wrote this book as an expansion of the service that I feel is important to provide to the local and surrounding community of health minded persons who might have misconceptions about yoga, that might feel that they don't fit the ideal image of the yoga practitioner and think that yoga is not for them. I wrote this book to share the unique method that I have developed that combines the best of physical therapy, fitness, and yoga with as many people as possible.

With this book I hope to reach people who are ready to take action to learn how to help reduce their own suffering, who have tried other methods and failed to have long term success, and who are eager to improve their long-term wellbeing by incorporating gentle therapeutic yoga lifestyle practices into their self-care regimen.

I wrote this book to share the gentle approach that I have developed over the last 40 years that considers the whole person, mind, body, and spirit and to share this unique approach to wellness that is influenced by the physical therapy, fitness, and yoga practices that I have learned, led, taught, shared, and embodied over the last forty years. The Therapeutic Astanga Method© that I regularly refer to as Therapeutic Yoga.

It is my hope that the persons reading this book might be able to make a start towards walking on a path towards wholeness by trying these practices and maybe this will lead them to something more.

This is my calling, my passion, and I have devoted my life to this work. I am looking forward to continuing to practice what I preach and share this method with as many people as are willing to hear or read about the benefits of therapeutic yoga.

CHAPTER 11

THERAPEUTIC YOGA PRACTICE

f you are reading this, congratulations, you have finished reading about Caroline's experience with therapeutic yoga that changed her life for the better. I do recognize that you might have just skipped to the back of the book to see what activities you can expect to find in this therapeutic yoga that make it so special. Whichever camp you fall in, I am happy that you are here.

This section lays out all the therapeutic yoga activities that made up the foundation of Caroline's program. These fundamental practices are relatively accessible to many persons, with some exceptions, of course. In my experience, they are important for persons who want to begin a therapeutic yoga practice and are a great way to get started. In this book, these activities were used to direct attention to developing focused concentration and breath awareness and efficiency, and to improving core stability, muscular endurance, functional strength, and mobility. I have also included some of my favorite awareness practices to inspire your participation to optimize breathing, improve standing posture, and encourage walking for exercise.

I recommend that you practice these activities three times per week at minimum. I also believe that doing these practices daily can be even more beneficial. Repeating these activities mindfully and on a regular basis can help you create your own breath-centered mindful movement meditation practice that I believe will benefit you for a lifetime.

The beneficial aspects of the practice that you create for yourself can be heightened by setting a positive intention towards yourself or others at the beginning of each session and can be used as a point of focus. I will often add a mantra that I repeat in my mind during the work, such as: "I am healing, I am strong, I am at peace,"or some variation of these phrases to help me set a powerful intention that I might then manifest as a reality in the present moment, as well as in the future.

These practices are important to master before progressing on to other therapeutic yoga postures that involve standing, balancing, seated, and other more challenging supine and prone positions. Do not be fooled. The Therapeutic Astanga Method© practices that you see here are not limited to individuals who suffer spine problems. These practices can be applied to a variety of conditions to help an individual connect with their whole self. These whole mind, body, and spirit practices do not discriminate. They are available to all who wish to step on the path towards wholeness. Remember, the only thing that you have to do is breathe.

A final reminder: if you would like a hard copy of this chapter for easy reference when doing the practice on your own, you can access a PDF that you can print out by going to TherapeuticYogaWorks.com. To reiterate, on the site you will also find videos of each posture and select practices that I designed to help you get started on your therapeutic yoga program.

Basic Tools for Your Therapeutic Yoga Practice

1. Yoga mat or towel
2. Non-stretch yoga strap
3. Cushion or rolled-up blanket for support
4. Willing spirit
5. Sense of humor

BREATHE TO REDUCE STRESS, MOBILIZE YOUR BODY, AND ACTIVATE THE RELAXATION RESPONSE.

1. Take a moment to settle into a comfortable position, either sitting or lying down.
2. Close your mouth, and bring your attention to your breath as it moves gently in and out of your nose. Breathe in, breathe out.

3. Focus your attention on your body as you rest. Allow your whole body to drop into the surface that supports you, and let go of any tension that you might be holding. Allow yourself to feel the softness that exists in your body. Breathe in, breathe out.

4. Bring your attention to the softness of your abdomen, the throat, the front of your torso and your pelvic floor. Allow these areas to move gently as you breathe. Notice the gentle expansion as you inhale and the gentle release inward as you exhale. Let your breath move you. There is no need to force or push. Breathe in, breathe out.

5. Place your right hand over your abdomen while you are breathing. Relax your shoulders, and visualize the internal organs that lie just inside the abdomen that are massaged and supported by the abdominal muscles, the pelvic floor, and the connective tissues that surround them. Feel the natural rhythm of your breath as it moves your body. Breathe in, breathe out.

6. Place your left hand on your rib cage and notice how it moves while you are breathing. Visualize the diaphragm that lies just inside your rib cage. This muscle melds with connective tissue and fascia along your thoracic spine. It lies below and is intimately woven into the underside of the cardiac sac that surrounds and protects your heart. Feel the natural rhythm of your breath moving your body. Breathe in, breathe out.

7. Move your right hand from your abdomen, and place it on your upper chest. Notice how it moves while you are breathing. Visualize the lungs and the heart that lie just inside the upper chest. These amazing organs coordinate the exchange of life-bringing oxygen that is extracted from the air, moved through the lung tissue, transported into the blood, and pumped by the heart throughout the entire body. Feel the natural rhythm of your breath moving your body. Breathe in, breathe out.

8. Feel the connection of the front, then the sides, and then the back of your rib cage and torso. Feel the sensation of protection that comes from this amazing bony structure. A structure that allows freedom of movement, maintains protection to the vital organs, and allows motion that massages and invigorates the organs within it. Feel how the natural rhythm of your breath massages and invigorates the organs and influences the gentle mobilization of the thoracic spine while at the same time protecting and vitalizing the internal organs. Breathe in, breathe out.

9. For the next few minutes, allow yourself to rest in this gentle and rhythmic massage. Allow yourself to feel the freedom

within the protection. Allow yourself to be present in this breath. To be present in this moment. Allow yourself to—just be.

10. Breathe in, breathe out.

Take a moment every day to stop and bring your attention to your breath. It is your SUPERPOWER!

DIAPHRAGMATIC BREATHING PRACTICE

Take a moment right now to settle into a comfortable position, either sitting in a supportive chair or lounger, or lying supported on your back with your legs also supported. Allow yourself to settle into your preferred position. Bring your awareness to the sensation of your body resting in the supportive position that you chose. Make any adjustments necessary to bring yourself into the most comfortable position possible. Settle.

Close your mouth, and bring your attention to your breath as it moves gently in and out of your nose. Breathe in, breathe out. Feel the sensation of the air that is moving through your nose and notice any qualities that are present in the air as it moves through your body. Breathe in, breathe out. What does the air feel like? Is it warm? Is it cool? Breathe in, breathe out. Is the air moist, or is it dry? Keep your attention on the qualities of the air as you breathe gently in and out. Bring your senses completely into your breath as you rest. Really feel the breath moving gently through your nose. Breathe in. Breathe out.

Now focus your attention on your body as you rest. Breathe in, breathe out. Allow your whole body to drop into the surface that supports you. Notice the sensation of the parts of your body that are contacting the surface that you are resting upon. Breathe in, breathe out. Allow yourself to rest in this supported position. Let go of any effort or muscular tension that you might be holding in your body. Breathe in, breathe out.

Allow yourself to feel the softness that exists in your body. Let go of any holding patterns that want to make your body rigid or stiff. Drop into the softness of your breath. Breathe in, breathe out. Bring your attention to the softness of your abdomen, the front of your torso, and your pelvic floor. Breathe in, breathe out. Allow these important areas to move gently as you breathe. Take notice of this gentle movement. The gentle expansion outward as you inhale and the gentle relaxation inward toward your center as you exhale. Let yourself melt into that softness. Allow that softness to move you. Breathe in, breathe out. Let the softness influence and gently move your body while you keep your attention on the gentle rhythm of your natural breath. Let your breath move you. Follow your breath as it moves naturally through and moves your body. Breathe in, breathe out. There is no need to force or push. Allow your breath to move naturally. Breathe in, breathe out.

Now place your right hand over your abdomen while you are breathing. Keep your shoulders relaxed and allow your elbow to stay supported while your hand rests lightly on your abdomen. Visualize the internal organs that lie just inside the abdomen that are influenced, massaged, and supported by the abdominal muscles, the pelvic floor, and the connective tissues that surround them. Feel the natural rhythm of your breath moving through your body. Keep your attention on maintaining a smooth and rhythmic breath. Breathe in, breathe out.

Bring your attention to your rib cage. Place your left hand on your rib cage and notice how it moves while you are breathing. Allow your elbow to stay supported while your hand rests lightly on your rib cage. Visualize the diaphragm that lies just inside your rib cage. How this beautiful muscle originates inside your rib cage and melds with connective tissue and fascia along your thoracic spine. t lies below and is intimately woven into the underside of the cardiac sac that surrounds and protects your heart. Feel the natural rhythm of your breath moving your body. Keep your attention on maintaining a smooth and rhythmic breath. Breathe in, breathe out.

Bring your attention to your upper chest. Move your right hand from your abdomen, and place it along your upper chest, and notice how it moves while you are breathing. Allow your elbow to stay supported while your hand rests lightly on your upper chest. Visualize the lungs and the heart that lie just inside the upper chest. How these amazing organs coordinate the exchange of life-bringing oxygen that is extracted from the air, moved through the lung tissue, transported into the blood, and pumped by the heart throughout the entire body. Feel the natural rhythm of your breath moving your body. Keep your attention on maintaining a smooth and rhythmic breath. Breathe in, breathe out.

Feel the connection of the front and then the sides and then the back of your rib cage and torso. Feel the sensation of protection that comes from this amazing bony and cartilaginous structure, and visualize a mobile protective structure. A structure that allows freedom of movement and yet maintains protection to the vital organs and allows motion that massages and invigorates the organs within it. Feel how the natural rhythm of your breath massages and invigorates the organs and influences the gentle mobilization of the thoracic spine while at the same time protecting and vitalizing the internal organs. Breathe in, breathe out.

For the next few minutes, allow yourself to rest in this gentle and rhythmic massage. Allow yourself to feel the freedom within the protection. Allow yourself to be present in this breath. To be present in this moment. Allow yourself to—just be. Breathe in, breathe out.

STANDING MOUNTAIN POSE

We begin in standing mountain pose, feet parallel and hip distance apart.

Close your mouth and breathe gently through your nose. Begin in the standing position in the standing mountain pose with your eyes open. Look forward and place your gaze on a point ahead of you that is not moving. Position your feet parallel and hip distance apart. Feel the weight even between the ball of the foot and the heel of the foot. Even between the right and left foot. Breathe.

Bring your awareness to your toes. Gently lift the toes while keeping the ball of your feet grounded to the mat to encourage the support of the muscular arch in each foot. Breathe.

Bring your attention to your knees. Activate the muscles in your lower body by creating a microscopic bend in both knees. Just enough to feel the support of the muscles in the front and back of your knees. Breathe.

Bring your attention to the position of your hips and spine. Feel your body weight settling evenly between the right and left hip. Feel a sense of elongation along your spine. Allow these areas to be positioned comfortably as you stand. Feel the gentle movement of your breath that influences your torso as you stand tall. Draw your shoulders gently back towards your spine and then down towards your pelvis. Feel the sensation of lengthening along the side of your neck as the shoulders move down and away from your ears. Breathe.

Feel an energetic lengthening of the arms that are resting alongside your body. Feel the energy moving through the arms all the way down to your fingertips. Feel the connection of your feet to the earth and begin to visualize your energetic life force combining with that of the earth and follow this force as it moves upward through the lower legs, thighs, through your hips and torso, along your spine, and upwards all the way to the top of your head. Feel your whole body simultaneously energized and calm. Stand tall in this position for 10 breaths. Fully aware of your surroundings and fully aware of maintaining smooth, gentle, and rhythmic breathing.

SUPINE MOUNTAIN POSE

If standing for a few minutes is difficult, you can work on developing the muscles that will help you by performing this alternative in the lying-down position.

1. Begin lying on your spine with your legs straight. Close your mouth and keep your attention on maintaining smooth and rhythmic breathing.
2. Firm the muscles on the front of your thighs while you position your arms (with wide fingers and palms) along the side of your body. Press the hands firmly into the mat and press the heels away from your body. Breathe.
3. Continue to breathe smoothly as you press the back of your head, wide-fingered hands, back of the arms, back of the thighs, and heels into the mat, and firm your buttocks.
4. Hold the position for five breaths.
5. Release.

THERAPEUTIC SUN SALUTATION©

This movement sequence is a variation of the Sun Salutation A that you might see in a traditional Hatha yoga practice. I created this variation to make the Sun Salutation more accessible to myself and to my clients who might be working with moderate limitations. I have shared this sequence with over 20 thousand people over the last 25 years and continue to share it because I have witnessed the benefit of mobilizing the major joints of the body as well as the process of grounding and connection that it provides the practitioner. I would be remiss if I did not mention the fact that it forms the foundation of the practices that help people move down to the floor and get back up. I try to share this practice with every person that I work with because I have witnessed its efficacy.

Begin in standing mountain posture with your hands at heart center, your feet parallel and hip distance apart. Check in to feel the weight even between both feet and keep the weight even between the ball of the foot and the heel on both sides. Lift your toes to begin to engage the muscles that support the structural arch in your feet. Then stretch the toes and relax them to rest on the mat.

During this and every activity, do the best that you can to breathe through your nose with your mouth closed. Do the best that you can.

Practicing gratitude: Focus your attention on something that you are grateful for today.

1. Inhale: Reach your arms out to the side and over your head.
    Exhale: Bring your hands down and back to your heart.
    Repeat three times.

2. Inhale: Reach your arms out to the side and over your head.
    Exhale: Bring your hands down and back to your heart while you bend your knees, and sit your bottom back as if moving to sit into a chair.
    Inhale: Straighten the legs as you reach your arms out to the side and over your head.
    Exhale: Bring your hands down and back to your heart while you bend your knees, and sit your bottom back as if moving to sit into a chair.
    Repeat three times.

3. Inhale: Reach up.
    Exhale: Bring the hands to the thighs.
    Repeat three times.

4. Inhale: Reach up.
    Exhale: Bring the hands to the thighs and hold them there. Stay in the bent knees position with your spine in neutral position.
    Prepare to move the spine.

5. Inhale: Extend the spine.
    Exhale: Flex and round through the spine.
    Repeat three times.

6. Inhale: Sweep your arms out to the sides and overhead while you straighten your knees to come back to upright standing.

Exhale: Bring your hands to your heart center to return to standing mountain.

7. Keep breathing smoothly as you widen the stance by stepping the feet wider than hip distance apart. Keep your knees and feet parallel, keep the weight even between the ball of the feet and the heels on each foot.

8. Inhale: Reach up.
   Exhale: Bend the hips, bend the knees, and drop your bottom as low as it feels comfortable (hands to thighs). Repeat three times.

9. **Inhale:** Reach up.
   Exhale: Sit your bottom back and if it feels right, try to touch the mat with your hands.
   Inhale: Reach up,
   Exhale: If you can, touch the mat.
   Repeat three times.

10. **Inhale:** Reach up.
    Exhale: Bring your hands down and touch the mat.
    Keep Breathing: Push the strong arms and hands (fingers and palms wide) into the mat.
    Walk the feet back into the downward-facing dog.
    The fingers are wide, the head is relaxed. Push yourself away from the floor.
    Don't worry if the heels are not touching the mat.
    Hold for three breaths.

11. **Keep Breathing:** From the downward facing dog position, bend the knees to bring them down the mat and sit your bottom back into child's pose to find the best resting position that honors your body.

12. **Hold for three breaths or more.**

13. **Keep Breathing:** Push into the mat/floor using the strength of your arms and hands (with your palms flat and fingers wide).
    Keep Breathing: Curl your toes under to help your feet move into position to make it easier to lift the knees off the mat. Press up into downward-facing dog. **Breathe.**

14. **Keep Breathing:** Widen the stance of your feet as you begin to walk your feet closer to your hands on the mat. Bend your

knees and move your feet towards your hands until your feet are completely in solid contact on the mat. Breathe.

15. **Keep Breathing:** Bring your hands to your thighs. **Breathe.**

16. Bring your torso to level with the earth, almost like a table-top. Hold here and breathe to help get your blood pressure to level out. **Breathe.**

17. **Inhale**: Slowly begin to push through the strength of your legs to straighten your body up back to the standing position as you sweep your arms overhead. Keep your eyes on a point of reference, a focal point to improve balance.
    Exhale: Bring your hands back to heart center and then rest your arms along the sides of your body.

Congratulations, you completed the Therapeutic Sun Salutation© and made it off the floor!

Therapeutic Yoga Works: Therapeutic Sun Salutation©

Inhale: Reach your arms out to the side and over your head.
Exhale: Bring your hands down and back to your heart.
Repeat three times.

Inhale: Reach your arms out to the side and over your head.
Exhale: Bring your hands down and back to your heart while you bend your knees and sit your bottom back as if moving to sit into a chair.
Inhale: Straighten the legs as you reach your arms out to the side and over your head.
Exhale: Bring your hands down and back to your heart while you bend your knees and sit your bottom back as if moving to sit into a chair.
Repeat three times.

1

Therapeutic Yoga Works: Therapeutic Sun Salutation©

Inhale: Reach up.
Exhale: Bring the hands to the thighs.
Repeat three times.

Inhale: Reach up.
Exhale: Bring the hands to the thighs and hold them there.
Stay in the bent knees position with your spine in neutral position.
Prepare to move the spine.

Inhale: Extend the spine.
Exhale: Flex and round through the spine.
Repeat three times.

2

Therapeutic Yoga Works: Therapeutic Sun Salutation©

Inhale: Sweep your arms out to the sides and overhead while you straighten your knees to come back to upright standing.
Exhale: Bring your hands to your heart center to return to standing mountain.

Keep breathing smoothly as you widen the stance by stepping the feet wider than hip distance apart. Keep your knees and feet parallel, keep the weight even between the ball of the feet and the heels on each foot.

Inhale: Reach up.
Exhale: Bend the hips, bend the knees, and drop your bottom as low as it feels comfortable (hands to thighs).
Repeat three times.

3

Therapeutic Yoga Works: Therapeutic Sun Salutation©

Inhale: Reach up.
Exhale: Sit your bottom back and if it feels right, try to touch the mat with your hands.
Inhale: Reach up,
Exhale: If you can, touch the mat.
Repeat three times.

Inhale: Reach up.
Exhale: Bring your hands down and touch the mat.
Keep Breathing: Push the strong arms and hands (fingers and palms wide) into the mat.
Walk the feet back into the downward-facing dog.
The fingers are wide, the head is relaxed. Push yourself away from the floor. Don't worry if the heels are not touching the mat.
Hold for three breaths.

4

Therapeutic Yoga Works: Therapeutic Sun Salutation©

Keep Breathing: From the downward facing dog position, bend the knees to bring them down the mat and sit your bottom back into child's pose to find the best resting position that honors your body. **Hold for three breaths or more.**

Keep Breathing: Push into the mat/floor using the strength of your arms and hands (with your palms flat and fingers wide).

Keep Breathing: Curl your toes under to help your feet move into position to make it easier to lift the knees off the mat. Press up into downward-facing dog. **Breathe.**

5

Therapeutic Yoga Works: Therapeutic Sun Salutation©

Keep Breathing: Widen the stance of your feet as you begin to walk your feet closer to your hands on the mat. Bend your knees and move your feet towards your hands until your feet are completely in solid contact on the mat. Breathe.

Keep Breathing: Bring your hands to your thighs. **Breathe.**
Bring your torso to level with the earth, almost like a tabletop. Hold here and breathe to help get your blood pressure to level out. **Breathe.**

Inhale: Slowly begin to push through the strength of your legs to straighten your body up back to the standing position as you sweep your arms overhead. Keep your eyes on a point of reference, a focal point to improve balance.
Exhale: Bring your hands back to heart center and then rest your arms along the sides of your body.
Congratulations, you completed the Therapeutic Sun Salutation© and made it off the floor!

6

FIRST HALF OF THE THERAPEUTIC SUN SALUTATION©

This movement sequence really is what it says it is. The first half of the movement sequence that I call the Therapeutic Sun Salutation© is a convenient practice when you want to warm the body and focus the mind, but you are either not ready or able to get down on to the floor safely on your own. This practice can be beneficial when you want to focus your attention on a standing practice that you can use on its own or as a precursor to other standing activities.

1. Begin in standing mountain posture with your hands at heart center and your feet parallel and hip distance apart. Check in to feel the weight even between both feet, and keep the weight even between the ball of the foot and the heel on both sides. Lift your toes to begin to engage the muscles that support the structural arch in the feet. Then stretch the toes and relax them to rest on the mat. During this and every activity, do the best that you can to breathe through your nose with your mouth closed.

2. Practicing gratitude: Focus your attention on something that you are grateful for today.

3. Inhale: Reach your arms out to the side and over your head.
   Exhale: Bring your hands down and back to your heart.
   Repeat three times.

4. Inhale: Reach your arms out to the side and over your head.
   Exhale: Bring your hands down and back to your heart while you bend your knees, and sit your bottom back as if moving to sit into a chair.
   Inhale: Straighten the legs as you reach your arms out to the side and over your head.
   Exhale: Bring your hands down and back to your heart while you bend your knees, and sit your bottom back as if moving to sit into a chair.
   Repeat three times.

5. Inhale: Reach up.
   Exhale: Bring the hands to the thighs.
   Repeat three times.

6. Inhale: Reach up.
    Exhale: Bring the hands to the thighs and hold them there.
    Stay in the knees-bent-with-spine-neutral position.
    Inhale: Extend the spine.
    Exhale: Flex and round through the spine.
    Repeat three times.

7. Inhale: Sweep your arms out to the sides and overhead while
    you straighten your knees to come back to upright stand ng.
    Exhale: Bring your hands to your heart center to return to
    standing mountain.

Therapeutic Yoga Works: Therapeutic Sun Salutation©

Inhale: Reach your arms out to the side and over your head.
Exhale: Bring your hands down and back to your heart.
Repeat three times.

Inhale: Reach your arms out to the side and over your head.
Exhale: Bring your hands down and back to your heart while you bend your knees and sit your bottom back as
if moving to sit into a chair.
Inhale: Straighten the legs as you reach your arms out to the side and over your head.
Exhale: Bring your hands down and back to your heart while you bend your knees and sit your bottom back as
if moving to sit into a chair.
Repeat three times.

1

Therapeutic Yoga Works: Therapeutic Sun Salutation©

Inhale: Reach up.
Exhale: Bring the hands to the thighs.
Repeat three times.

Inhale: Reach up.
Exhale: Bring the hands to the thighs and hold them there.
Stay in the bent knees position with your spine in neutral position.
Prepare to move the spine.

Inhale: Extend the spine.
Exhale: Flex and round through the spine.
Repeat three times.

2

Therapeutic Yoga Works: First Half of the Therapeutic Sun Salutation©

Inhale: Sweep your arms out to the sides and overhead while you straighten your knees to come back to upright standing.
Exhale: Bring your hands to your heart center to return to standing mountain.

3

SHORT FORM THERAPEUTIC SUN SALUTATION©

This movement sequence assumes that you have been practicing the Therapeutic Sun Salutation©. It will get easier with consistent practice. During this and every activity, do the best that you can to focus your attention on breathing through your nose with your mouth closed.

1. Begin in a wide stance by stepping the feet wider than hip distance apart. Keep your knees and feet parallel and keep the weight even between the balls of the feet and the heel on each foot.

2. Inhale: Reach up.
    Exhale: Bring your hands down onto the mat, keeping your fingers and palms wide and in firm contact with the mat.
    Now push with strong arms and hands into the mat.
    Walk the feet back into downward-facing dog.
    The fingers are wide, the head is relaxed, and you are pushing the floor away from you. Don't worry if the heels are not touching the mat.
    Breathe!

3. From the downward-facing dog, bend the knees to bring them down the mat. Sit your bottom back towards your heels to move into the child's pose.
    Breathe!

Therapeutic Yoga Works: Short Form Therapeutic Sun Salutation©

Keep breathing smoothly as you widen the stance by stepping the feet wider than hip distance apart. Keep your knees and feet parallel, keep the weight even between the ball of the feet and the heels on each foot.

Inhale: Reach up.
Exhale: Bend the hips, bend the knees, and drop your bottom as low as it feels comfortable (hands to thighs).
Repeat three times.

Inhale: Reach up.
Exhale: Sit your bottom back and if it feels right, try to touch the mat with your hands.
Inhale: Reach up,
Exhale: If you can, touch the mat.
Repeat three times.

1

Therapeutic Yoga Works: Short Form Therapeutic Sun Salutation©

Inhale: Reach up.
Exhale: Bring your hands down and touch the mat.
Keep Breathing: Push the strong arms and hands (fingers and palms wide) into the mat.
Walk the feet back into the downward-facing dog.
The fingers are wide, the head is relaxed. Push yourself away from the floor. Don't worry if the heels are not touching the mat.
Hold for three breaths.

Keep Breathing: From the downward facing dog position, bend the knees to bring them down the mat and sit your bottom back into child's pose to find the best resting position that honors your body.
Hold for three breaths or more.

2

Therapeutic Yoga Works: Short Form Therapeutic Sun Salutation©

Keep Breathing: Push into the mat/floor using the strength of your arms and hands (with your palms flat and fingers wide).

Keep Breathing: Curl your toes under to help your feet move into position to make it easier to lift the knees off the mat. Press up into downward-facing dog. **Breathe.**

Keep Breathing: Widen the stance of your feet as you begin to walk your feet closer to your hands on the mat. Bend your knees and move your feet towards your hands until your feet are completely in solid contact on the mat. Breathe.
Keep Breathing: Bring your hands to your thighs. **Breathe.**
Bring your torso to level with the earth, almost like a tabletop. Hold here and breathe to help get your blood pressure to level out. **Breathe.**

3

Therapeutic Yoga Works: Short Form Therapeutic Sun Salutation©

Inhale: Slowly begin to push through the strength of your legs to straighten your body up back to the standing position as you sweep your arms overhead. Keep your eyes on a point of reference, a focal point to improve balance.

Exhale: Bring your hands back to heart center and then rest your arms along the sides of your body. Congratulations, you completed the Therapeutic Sun Salutation© and made it off the floor!

GETTING UP OFF THE FLOOR

This activity is harder than it looks to the casual observer and more important than most people realize. If you end up on the floor and you can't get up, it could lead to serious health complications and even an untimely death. We can help to reduce these complications by keeping our bodies mobile and strong enough to do this practice on a regular basis.

1. Close your mouth and keep your attention on maintaining smooth and rhythmic breathing.

2. If you are lying on your back, bend your knees, roll onto your side, and then onto your stomach. Breathe while you are doing this.

3. Come up onto your elbows and see how that feels. Push into your elbows and hands to lift your hips off the floor and move onto your hands and knees. Breathe.

4. Push into the mat/floor using the strength of your arms and hands (with your palms flat and fingers wide). Keep breathing.

5. Curl your toes under to help your feet move into position to make it easier to lift the knees off the mat. Press up into downward-facing dog. Breathe.

6. Widen the stance of your feet as you begin to walk your feet closer to your hands on the mat. Bend your knees and move your feet towards your hands until your feet are completely in solid contact on the mat. Breathe.

7. Bring your hands to your thighs. Breathe.

8. Bring your torso to level with the earth, almost like a table-top. Hold here, and breathe to help get your blood pressure to level out. Breathe.

9. Then slowly begin to push through the strength of your legs to straighten your body up back to the standing position. Keep your eyes on a point of reference, a focal point to improve balance. Breathe.

10. Congratulations, you made it off the floor!

Therapeutic Yoga Works: Getting Off the Floor. It Could Save Your Life!

PLEASE BE MINDFUL! This activity is more challenging than it looks. Review each step before attempting. **Do not try this by yourself if you have not been on the floor in some time.** You can begin working on strengthening to get your hips and torso to move off the surface when lying on your stomach on a firm and wide bed. **When in doubt of your physical abilities, contact a physical therapist for assistance.** While you are at it, show them these instructions.

Close your mouth and keep your attention on maintaining smooth and rhythmic breathing. If you are lying on your back, bend your knees, roll onto your side, and then onto your stomach. **Breathe while you are doing this.** Come up onto your elbows and see how that feels.

...

Keep Breathing: Push into your elbows and hands to lift your hips off the floor and move onto your hands and knees. **Breathe.** Push into the mat/floor using the strength of your arms and hands (with your palms flat and fingers wide). **Keep breathing.** Curl your toes under to help your feet move into position to make it easier to lift the knees off the mat.*** Press up into downward-facing dog. **Breathe.**

***This is harder than it looks. If you are not able lift your knees up off the floor, try using a very solid couch or sturdy chair that is backed up against a wall to pull up into kneeling to help get you up. **Remember to contact a physical therapist. We are nice people who really want to help you get stronger.**

1

Therapeutic Yoga Works: Getting Off the Floor. It Could Save Your Life!

Keep Breathing: Widen the stance of your feet as you begin to walk your feet closer to your hands on the mat. Bend your knees and move your feet towards your hands until your feet are completely in solid contact on the mat. **Breathe.**

Keep Breathing: Bring your hands to your thighs. **Breathe.**
Bring your torso to level with the earth, almost like a tabletop. **Hold here and breathe** to help get your blood pressure to level out. **Breathe.**

Keep Breathing: Slowly begin to push through the strength of your legs to straighten your body up back to the standing position. Keep your eyes on a point of reference, a focal point to improve balance.
Bring your hands back to heart center and say a word of thanks to your body, mind, and spirit, then rest your arms along the sides of your body.
Congratulations, you did something that is way harder than it looks. You made it off the floor!

2

QUADRUPED SETUP

This activity helps to develop the strength and stability of the muscles that support the shoulder blade as it connects to the area along the rib cage. This area is important to encouraging the stability that is important when we are developing the strength of the shoulder girdle and the neck. It is an important foundational activity that will benefit all practitioners on and off the yoga mat for the long term.

1. Start by positioning your body on your hands and knees.
2. Close your mouth and keep your attention on maintaining smooth and rhythmic breathing.
3. Widen your palms and fingers on the mat. Feel the weight even between both hands.
4. Keep the weight even between the ball of the hand and the heel of the hand.
5. Notice the weight of your body even between the right and left knee.
6. Engage the muscles in your arms, and press them firmly into the mat.
7. Move your shoulders away from your ears.
8. Look down and focus your gaze on a point between your hands on the mat.
9. Press the back of your head and move the area between your shoulder blades towards the ceiling.
10. Hold this position for five breaths.
11. Release.

DOWNWARD-FACING DOG

This is a popular yoga posture that has many benefits including helping to improve upper body strength, shoulder girdle range of motion and stability, and positively influencing the mobility of the spine, back of the thighs, and lower legs. This posture also provides an opportunity for practicing a moderate inversion allowing the practitioner to change their perspective. Getting upside down is not for everyone. (See Precautions for Practicing Variations to Supported Inversions on page 90.

1. Start in the quadruped posture on your hands and knees.
2. Close your mouth and keep your attention on maintaining smooth and rhythmic breathing.
3. Draw the shoulders away from your ears and press the back of your head and ribs gently towards the ceiling.
4. Create a microscopic bend in your elbows to help you to activate the strength of your arms as you press your wide-fingered hands firmly into the mat.
5. Curl the toes under to prepare the position of your feet.
6. Press the floor away from your body as you lift your knees off the mat.
7. Straighten your knees, and move your hips up into the air to feel a stretch at the back of the thighs and lower legs.
8. Lengthen through the spine, and move the back of your head gently in the same direction towards the ceiling as your ribs.
9. Focus your gaze on your feet or a point that lies behind you on the yoga mat.
10. Hold this position for five breaths.
11. Bend the knees and return to the supported position in quadruped.
12. Take rest in child's pose.

CAT/COW

This movement practice is effective at gently mobilizing the thoracic spine, internal organs, and nervous system and also can have a positive influence on the structures that are influenced by efficient breathing, such as the vocal, abdominal, and pelvic diaphragms.

1. Begin by starting in the quadruped posture on your hands and knees, active in pressing your body away from the mat.
2. Close your mouth and keep your attention on maintaining smooth and rhythmic breathing.
3. Inhale and begin to extend your spine by dropping your abdomen towards the mat while your chest opens forward and your tailbone lifts up behind you. Feel the strength in your back muscles and the length of your abdominal muscles.
4. Exhale and begin to flex your spine, tucking your head, rounding your spine, and tucking your tailbone under your body. Feel the strength of your abdominal muscles and the length of your back muscles.
5. Repeat five times.
6. Rest.

THREAD THE NEEDLE

This posture has the potential to positively influence the mobility of the thoracic (rib) cage and spine, facilitate a gentle massage of the internal organs, and can support the mobility necessary in the thoracic region to encourage natural, smooth, and relaxed breathing.

1. Begin by starting in the quadruped posture on your hands and knees.
2. Close your mouth and keep your attention on maintaining smooth and rhythmic breathing.
3. Inhale, and lift your right arm straight out to the right side and up towards the ceiling.
4. Exhale, and move your right arm down and underneath your body towards the left knee.
5. Allow the right shoulder, the back of the right hand and arm, and the right side of your forehead (if possible) to rest on the mat.
6. Keep breathing, and feel the strength of your arm muscles as you press the right shoulder and the back of the right hand and arm firmly into the mat.
7. Feel the lengthening of the muscles along your torso, side waist, and shoulder as you hold this position for five breaths.
8. Release and raise the right arm back out from under your body, moving it up and out to the side. Then place the right hand back down on the mat.
9. Repeat on the left side.

CHILD'S POSE

This posture is considered a resting pose, but may not be as easy as it looks for individuals who are new to its practice. It has the potential to positively influence the natural mobility of the ankles, hips, spine, and shoulders. It also encourages the flexibility of the muscles along the front of the ankles, front of the thighs, buttocks, and spine. With practice, the practitioner can develop the range of motion that can make this posture a relaxing experience, and it can eventually become the resting pose that it was intended to be.

1. Begin in the quadruped position on your hands and knees with your toes pointed behind you (plantar flex the ankles).
2. Close your mouth and keep your attention on maintaining smooth and rhythmic breathing.
3. Move your hips back towards your heels.
4. Cross your forearms to rest your forehead on the back of your crossed forearms, or allow your forehead to rest on the mat, and stretch your arms along the side of your body.
5. Breathe, and bring your awareness to the sensation of stretch that you might be experiencing along the front of your thighs, back of your hips, and along the spine.
6. Hold this position for five breaths.
7. Release.

SIDE-LYING WITH PILLOWS FOR SUPPORT

This position is beneficial for those who are in need of support for the low back and hip area when in the side-lying position. Side-lying may benefit those practitioners who need a break or a change of position when lying on their back or on their stomach becomes uncomfortable.

1. Begin lying on your spine, knees bent with feet hip distance apart. Feel the weight even between the ball of the foot and the heel on both feet.
2. Close your mouth and keep your attention on maintaining smooth and rhythmic breathing.
3. Bring your awareness to the position of your body on the mat.
4. Place a small pillow or rolled towel between your knees for support.
5. Roll onto the side of your body, keeping the rolled towel/pillow in place between the knees. (The height of the pillow will attempt to allow the thighs to be supported so that they are level.)
6. Place another small pillow or rolled towel along the side and under the head for support. (The height of the pillow will allow the head to be supported in a neutral alignment to reduce stress to the neck and shoulder region.)
7. Position the arms for comfort. Use of a small pillow at the abdomen can help support the arm that is closer to the ceiling when in side-lying position.
8. Hold for a few breaths, then rest.
9. Use this side-lying supported position to take a break from prone or supine positions during therapeutic yoga practice.
10. Use this option of pillow support to help make side-sleeping more comfortable, as needed.

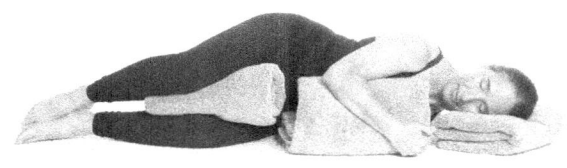

THERAPEUTIC BRIDGE POSE ONE

This posture is effective at gently introducing a beginning strength to the whole back side of the body while also helping to lengthen the tissues along the front side of the body. The practitioner is able to begin to gently develop the strength of the muscles of the spine extensors, hips, thighs, shoulders and arms that are important in maintaining upright neutral alignment and "good" posture. It is the very beginning of a backward bend and, in my opinion, one of the best postures that you can do for maintaining a healthy body.

1. Begin lying on your spine, knees bent with feet hip distance apart. Feel the weight even between the ball of the foot and the heel on both feet.
2. Close your mouth and keep your attention on maintaining smooth and rhythmic breathing.
3. Bring your awareness to the position of your body on the mat.
4. Lengthen your spine on the mat. Allow the back of your head, shoulders, hips, and feet to connect to the mat.
5. Stretch your arms along the side of your body, widen the fingers, and stretch the palms flat on the mat.
6. Press the hands, arms, feet, and back of the head lightly into the mat.
7. Firm the buttocks, and begin to lift the hips.
8. Keep the arms pressing into the mat.
9. Breathe.
10. Hold this position for five breaths.
11. Release.

SUPINE KNEES-TO-CHEST STRETCH

This posture is effective at stretching the muscles along the back of the hips, buttocks, and spine as well as strengthening the muscles of the front of the body, such as the abdominals and hip flexors. It is a popular posture that many people enjoy to help improve the mobility of their lower spine and to help reduce muscle tension that might have accumulated there.

1. Begin lying on your spine, knees bent with feet hip distance apart. Feel the weight even between the ball of the foot and the heel on both feet.
2. Close your mouth and keep your attention on maintaining smooth and rhythmic breathing.
3. Bring your awareness to the position of your body on the mat.
4. Lengthen your spine on the mat. Allow the back of your head, shoulders, hips, and feet to connect to the mat.
5. Bend your right knee, and begin to move it towards your chest by holding onto your thigh with both arms or a solid strap.
6. Hold this position while you breathe gently and invite your left knee towards your chest.
7. Hold both thighs with your arms or a solid strap.
8. Feel the sensation of stretch along the backside of your hips and along your spine.
9. Hold this position for five breaths.
10. Release, and repeat as comfortable.

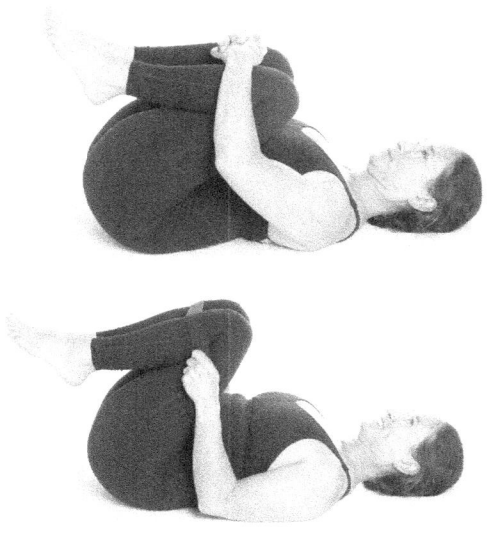

SUPINE SINGLE-KNEE-TO-CHEST STRETCH WITH TWIST

This movement activity helps to mobilize the hips, thighs, and spine when used regularly. It also helps to encourage thoracic spine mobility that can encourage efficient breathing when practiced with awareness on a regular basis.

1. Begin lying on your spine, knees bent with feet hip distance apart. Feel the weight even between the ball of the foot and the heel on both feet.
2. Close your mouth and keep your attention on maintaining smooth and rhythmic breathing.
3. Bring your awareness to the position of your body on the mat.
4. Lengthen your spine on the mat. Allow the back of your head, shoulders, hips, and feet to connect to the mat.
5. Lift your right foot off the mat, and begin to move your knee towards your chest by holding onto your thigh with both arms or a solid strap.
6. Straighten the left knee on the mat, and press the heel of your leg away from your center.
7. Firm the thigh muscles, and dorsiflex the ankle of the left leg by moving the top of your foot and toes towards your shin.
8. Hold the position for five breaths.
9. Reach the left hand to the right thigh, and invite the right thigh to move across the body towards the left side.
10. Anchor the right shoulder, arm, and wide-fingered hand onto the mat for support.
11. Turn your head to look over to the right side.
12. Hold this position for five breaths.
13. Release, and repeat on the left side.

SUPINE HAMSTRING STRETCH WITH STRAP

This posture helps to develop mobility and flexibility along the back of the foot, ankle, calf, hamstring, and gluteal and lower back areas of the body, as well as strengthen the muscles along the front of the lower leg, thigh, and hip flexors. The use of the strap to support the lower extremity that can help the nervous system "trust" that the body is being handled mindfully and can create an opportunity for the shoulder girdle to practice stabilizing and potentially strengthen the connection for the upper body as it relates to the rib cage and torso.

1. Begin lying on your spine, knees bent with feet hip distance apart. Feel the weight even between the ball of the foot and the heel on both feet.
2. Close your mouth and keep your attention on maintaining smooth and rhythmic breathing.
3. Bring your awareness to the position of your body on the mat.
4. Lengthen your spine on the mat. Allow the back of your head, shoulders, hips, and feet to connect to the mat.
5. Bend your right knee, and place a strap around the ball of the foot.
6. Hold on to the strap evenly on each side, with the right and left hands separate.
7. Breathe while you begin to firm the muscles in the front of the right thigh to straighten the right knee.
8. Keep the left knee bent with the left foot on the mat, or allow the left knee to straighten out on the mat.
9. Firm the muscle on the front of both thighs, and press your heels away from your body while you hold the thighs straight.
10. Engage the muscles in the left buttock and hip area.
11. Hold this position for five breaths.
12. Release, and repeat on the left side.

 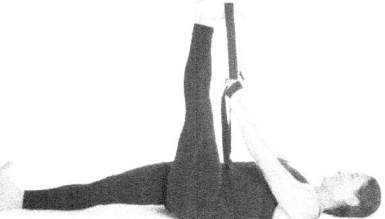

SUPINE HIP ADDUCTOR/ABDUCTOR STRETCH

This posture helps to encourage the mobility of the hip joint, and along with the next few hip mobility activities, it can play a major role in helping a person keep their functional independence for the long term. In my experience, limited motion within the hip joint is a leading cause of challenges that can lead to lower back pain and can also negatively impact the knee joint. Many adults gradually lose the normal range of motion in their hip joint due to leading a sedentary lifestyle and not performing these types of activities. I hope to change that in all persons that I work with.

1. Begin lying on your spine, knees bent with feet hip distance apart. Feel the weight even between the ball of the foot and the heel on both feet.
2. Close your mouth and keep your attention on maintaining smooth and rhythmic breathing.
3. Bring your awareness to the position of your body on the mat.
4. Lengthen your spine on the mat. Allow the back of your head, shoulders, hips, and feet to connect to the mat.
5. Bend your left knee and place a strap around the ball of the foot.
6. Hold on to the strap evenly on each side, with the right and left hands separate.
7. Breathe while you begin to firm the muscles in front of the left thigh to straighten the left knee.
8. Keep the right knee bent with the right foot on the mat, or allow the right knee to straighten out on the mat.
9. Firm the muscle on the front of both thighs, and press your heels away from your body while you hold the thighs straight.
10. Engage the muscles in the right buttock and hip area.
11. Now take both sides of the strap into the left hand.
12. Invite the left thigh to move out to the left side.
13. Place your right hand on the front of the right hip to support the hips to stay level on the mat.
14. Press the heels energetically away from your center.
15. Hold this position for five smooth and rhythmic breaths.

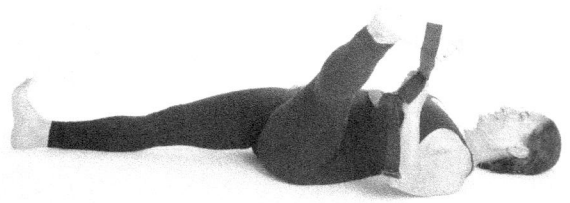

SUPINE HIP ADDUCTOR/ABDUCTOR STRETCH (CONTINUED)

16. Keep breathing smoothly while you move the left thigh back to center.
17. Switch hands so that the right hand is holding the straps.
18. Begin to invite the left thigh gently towards the right side.
19. Only move to the right as much as you can keep both hips stable and supported on the mat.
20. Feel a gentle stretch along the left side of the hip and thigh.
21. If you are able to keep your breath smooth and rhythmic while you do it, allow your left hip to move off of the mat to invite the body into a deeper stretch.
22. Hold the position for five breaths.
23. Maintain smooth and rhythmic breathing as you return to center.
24. Release, and repeat on the right side.

SUPINE HIP INTERNAL ROTATION

This is another very important motion that can positively influence a person's mobility, reduce restrictions in the hip, and potentially contribute to healthy low back and knee joints. The direction to keep the ankles held in dorsiflexion is important in that the position can help to create more space within the middle part of the knee joint to help keep the ligament structures free from stress while performing the important activity.

1. Begin lying on your spine, knees bent with feet hip distance apart. Feel the weight even between the balls of the feet and the heels.
2. Close your mouth and keep your attention on maintaining smooth and rhythmic breathing.
3. Bring your awareness to the position of your body on the mat.
4. Lengthen your spine on the mat. Allow the back of your head, shoulders, arms, hands, hips, and feet to connect to the mat.
5. Keep the knees bent and thighs vertical as you step both feet off to the sides of the mat. Move them as far away from center as possible.
6. Dorsiflex the ankles and extend the toes. Hold the foot and ankle in this position throughout the entire hip rotation stretch.
7. Invite the thighs to fall toward the center so that the knees almost touch.
8. Feel the stretch along the outer hips and along the upper thighs.
9. Hold this position for five breaths.
10. Release, and return the thighs to vertical, which is the resting position.

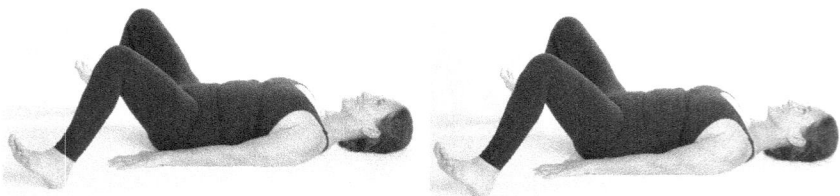

SUPINE BUTTERFLY PRESS HIP EXTERNAL ROTATION

This is another important hip mobility and strengthening activity that also encourages core stability. This posture is not easy, but along with the other postures that influence the hip, it can be an important part of a person's long-term functional mobility training program.

1. Begin lying on your spine, knees bent with feet hip distance apart. Feel the weight even between the ball of the foot and the heel on both feet.
2. Close your mouth and keep your attention on maintaining smooth and rhythmic breathing.
3. Bring your awareness to the position of your body on the mat.
4. Lengthen your spine on the mat. Allow the back of your head, shoulders, arms, hands, hips, and feet to connect to the mat.
5. Step the feet together, and begin to drop the thighs out to the side.
6. Press the soles of the feet together.
7. Firm the muscles of your buttocks, and press your arms and hands firmly into the mat.
8. Lift the hips off the mat.
9. Hold this position for five breaths.
10. Release and return to resting position.

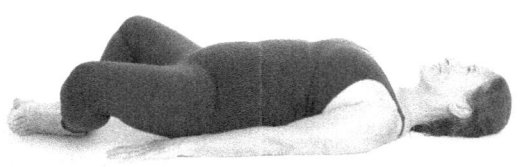

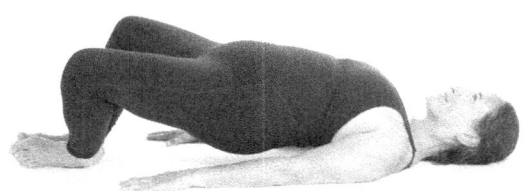

SUPINE FIGURE-FOUR STRETCH

This is a posture has been loved or hated by the people with hip mobility restrictions that I have worked with over the years. It is one of the best methods for encouraging flexibility to the piriformis (often referred to as the "pain in the butt") muscle. Those who are suffering from sciatic pain can benefit from putting this activity into their daily movement practices. This posture joins the other hip mobility activities that I have listed as important to encouraging a person's long-term functional mobility.

1. Begin lying on your spine, knees bent with feet hip distance apart. Feel the weight even between the ball of the foot and the heel on both feet.
2. Close your mouth and keep your attention on maintaining smooth and rhythmic breathing.
3. Bring your awareness to the position of your body on the mat.
4. Lengthen your spine on the mat. Allow the back of your head, shoulders, hips, and feet to connect to the mat.
5. Bend your right knee, and hug it into your chest.
6. Dorsiflex the right ankle and extend your toes.
7. Cross the right ankle over the left thigh.
8. Activate the muscles in the right hip as you invite the right thigh to rotate out to the side in a moment of external rotation.
9. Be aware to keep the back of both hip bones even on the mat.
10. Hold the position for five breaths.
11. Keep the breath smooth, and begin to lift the left thigh towards your torso.
12. Support the left thigh with your arms or a strap (right arm looped between the thighs) to move into a deeper stretch for the right hip.
13. Hold this position for five breaths.
14. Release, and repeat on the left side.

SUPINE SPINE TWIST

This movement is one of the most popular postures that I share with my clients and therapeutic yoga students. It is also one of my top 10 favorites, but then it is true that I have about a hundred top 10 favorite therapeutic yoga postures. I appreciate this posture for the way that it influences the thoracic spine towards improved mobility and for the positive influence that it can have on stimulating the autonomic nervous system and vagus nerve that communicates information between the brain and the internal organs. This posture is recognized for helping balance the optimum functioning of the gut and intestines. I love to share that this posture is an excellent way to gently mobilize and massage your internal organs and help them to function as nature intended. Yes, I am referring to pooping. I think that everyone should do some variation of this posture every day.

1. Begin lying on your spine, knees bent with feet hip distance apart. Feel the weight even between the ball of the foot and the heel on both feet.
2. Close your mouth and keep your attention on maintaining smooth and rhythmic nasal breathing.
3. Bring your awareness to the position of your body on the mat.
4. Lengthen your spine on the mat. Allow the back of your head, shoulders, hips, and feet to connect to the mat.
5. Lift your right thigh, cross it mindfully over your left thigh, and engage the muscles along your inner thighs by squeezing them together. Breathe.
6. Anchor your right hand, arm, and shoulder firmly on the mat next to your body.
7. Invite the thighs to move towards your left side so that you can begin to feel a gentle stretch along the right side of your right hip and the right side of your waist. Move as far to the left as you are able to keep the breath smooth and gentle, and both shoulders level on the mat.
8. Hold this position for five breaths.
9. Mindfully, move your thighs back to the center and uncross your thighs. Breathe.
10. Keep breathing smoothly, and repeat this mindful movement on the other side.

PRONE HIP AND SPINE EXTENSION WITH PILLOW SUPPORT

This posture is important for those who have shortened hip flexors to the degree that the hip joint is unable to extend to a neutral position without creating discomfort at either the low back or at the front of the hip joint. Using body weight to passively stretch the joints of the body is one of my favorite functional ways to improve motion for the long term. The pillow for support is crucial to creating support that allows a gentle progression in motion that can be more comfortable and, in my experience, more effective for the long term. The size of the pillow for support is gradually reduced over time until the hip is able to tolerate the position without support.

1. Begin on your hands and knees (in the quadruped position).
2. Close your mouth and keep your attention on maintaining smooth and rhythmic breathing.
3. Position a folded bath towel or small pillow in the center of the yoga mat so that it will lie under your abdomen for support when you move onto your stomach from the hands-and-knees position.
4. Position yourself so that your abdomen is over the folded towel/pillow.
5. Bend your elbows to move down onto your elbows and knees, and gradually move your body down to the mat to allow the abdomen and front of hips to rest on the folded towel/pillow.
6. Lie on your abdomen supported by the folded towel/pillow while you rest your forehead on the back of your crossed forearms.
7. Allow your body to settle into this supported position while you focus your attention on maintaining smooth and rhythmic breathing.
8. Stay in this position for 20 breaths or as it feels comfortable.
9. Gently move yourself off the support by rolling to the side to gradually move off of the folded towel/pillow and into a side-lying or seated supported position.
10. Rest.

PRONE SPINE EXTENSION

This activity is important to helping a person maintain the normal range of motion of the hip and spine while using body weight and positioning to encourage balance within the joints, which can improve the ability to maintain upright posture and reduce limitation and pain in surrounding joints.

1. Begin lying on your abdomen, forehead resting on the back of the crossed forearms, thighs and lower legs stretched out along the mat.
2. Close your mouth and keep your attention on maintaining smooth and rhythmic breathing.
3. Feel the sensation of the front of your body supported on the mat as you press the tops of your feet into the mat, and engage the muscles at the front of the thighs and along the back of your hips.
4. Bring your attention to the parts of your torso that are being moved by the breath as you are energetically lengthened along on the mat while you move your shoulders down and away from your ears, towards your hips.
5. Hold in this extended position for five breaths.
6. Release.

PRONE HIP EXTENSION

This activity is a progression from the prone spine extension and is designed to strengthen the gluteal and hamstring and also the spine extensor muscles along the back. Getting strength and motion in this area is important to bringing hip and spine mobility closer to balance.

1. Begin lying on your abdomen, forehead resting on the back of the crossed forearms, thighs and lower legs stretched out along the mat.
2. Close your mouth and keep your attention on maintaining smooth and rhythmic breathing.
3. Feel the sensation of the front of your body supported on the mat, as you press the tops of your feet into the mat and engage the muscles at the front of the thighs and along the back of your hips.
4. Bring your attention to the parts of your torso that are being moved by the breath as you are energetically lengthened along on the mat while you move your shoulders down and away from your ears, towards your hips.
5. Feel the breath moving your torso and engage the right thigh as you begin to lift the lengthened thigh away from the mat.
6. Hold in this lifted position for five breaths.
7. Release, and repeat on the left side.

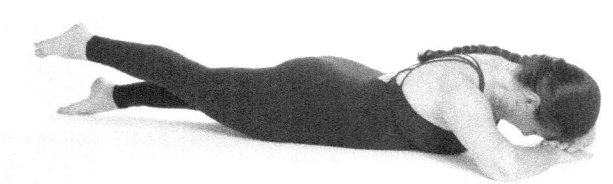

SPHINX POSTURE

This posture is a progression of the prone spine extension activity that then encourages hyperextension that a healthy spine should be able to move into for improved functional range of motion to the entire body. It is not as easy as it looks at first, but with gradual progression, a person can see and feel the benefit from being able to move into this position with grace. Please note that many people will feel slight increase in tension in the low back at their individual full extended position. This is normal and should resolve as soon as you release from the position and return back to the resting position.

1. Begin lying on your abdomen, forehead resting on the back of the crossed forearms and legs stretched out along the mat.
2. Close your mouth and keep your attention on maintaining smooth and rhythmic breathing.
3. Feel the sensation of the front of your body supported on the mat.
4. Bring your attention to the parts of your body that are being moved as you are lengthened along on the mat.
5. Move your shoulders down away from your ears and towards your hips, and breathe.
6. Keep your elbows in position as you stretch your forearms forward on the mat.
7. Keep breathing as you bring your elbows to rest underneath your shoulders, and align your forearms close to parallel to each other while you begin to lift your chest off of the mat.
8. Feel the sensation of strength along your arms, shoulder girdle, and upper middle back, and the stretch along the front of your body as you extend your torso into the posture.
9. Hold in this lifted position for five breaths.
10. Release and rest.

SUPPORTED LEGS UP THE WALL WITH A BLANKET FOR SUPPORT

This posture is a favorite because it feels so good to get gently upside down when the legs are supported up against a sturdy surface like a wall or a heavy piece of furniture. When we don't have a sturdy wall available, we can use a blanket to elevate the hips. This makes the posture portable so that you don't need to have a wall. The position that the blanket puts your pelvis in when it is elevated on the blanket allows the legs to remain up in the air with minimal effort (at least for a majority of persons). If you notice that you are working hard to keep the legs up in the air, then that is a sign that it is not time to have the legs extended up in the air for this posture. You might feel better keeping the knees bent.

1. Begin lying on your spine, knees bent with feet hip distance apart. Feel the weight even between the ball of the foot and the heel on both feet.
2. Close your mouth and keep your attention on maintaining smooth and rhythmic breathing.
3. Bring your awareness to the position of your body on the mat.
4. Lengthen your spine on the mat. Allow the back of your head, shoulders, arms, hands, hips, and feet to connect to the mat.
5. Have a small pillow or rolled-up blanket/towel within reach.
6. Press the feet and arms into the mat as you lift your hips up to position the rolled blanket/towel underneath your hips.
7. Allow the low back to drop gently towards the mat while the hips are lifted.
8. Lift your right leg up towards your chest. Follow with your left leg.
9. Feel the gentle stretch along the low back. This should feel good.
10. Straighten the right and then the left knee so that your legs are elevated with your feet reaching to the ceiling.
11. In the optimum position, you are not working hard to keep the legs balanced as they are positioned.
12. Continue to breathe gently.
13. Let your body rest in this lifted and supported position for a few minutes.
14. Reverse the process to release the pose.
15. Rest.

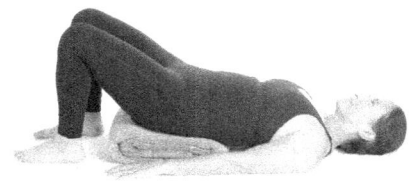

FOOT AND ANKLE RANGE OF MOTION

These fundamental movement practices are not often appreciated for the role that they play in helping us move freely in our daily lives. Many of us put shoes on our feet to support them but may not realize that there are close to thirty muscles that help us to coordinate the actions of the foot and ankle, and that's just for one side. These activities are designed to draw out the natural actions of the muscles that create movement, stabilizing and propelling us forward in walking, running, squatting, etc. When these muscles are in good condition and doing their assigned jobs, they can stabilize, mobilize, and energize the body owner, and they are able to play an important role in giving us information about the condition of the nervous and cardiac systems, and play a role in improving balance and coordination, as well as helping to reduce the risk of falls. Some people have spent years wearing shoes all day, without ever removing them to inspect the toes and the underside of their feet. I hope that you will make this activity part of your daily routine. It will be worth your time, attention, and effort.

Note: Of all of the therapeutic yoga activities that I lead my clients through, the foot and ankle motion activities are the ones that I notice most everyone holding their breath as they attempt to perform them. I recommend that you take your time, move slowly, and move through the greatest amount of motion that you are comfortable with. Notice when you might be holding your breath, and if you do hold your breath, don't worry, you haven't failed. You actually have succeeded in your efforts towards practicing mindfulness. Just return to your rhythmic breathing while you do the best that you can to complete the activities. Enjoy!

1. This activity can be performed while sitting reclined with legs stretched out ahead of you or while in the supported legs-up-the-wall posture. Find the most comfortable and supportive position.
2. Close your mouth and keep your attention on maintaining smooth and rhythmic breathing.
3. Begin by alternating flexing and extending your toes.
4. Now, hold the toes in the flexed position while you move from the ankle joint to make large circles with your feet five times. First in one direction, then the other.
5. Rest.
6. Now, hold the toes in the extended position while you move from the ankle joint to make large circles with your feet five times. First in one direction, then the other.
7. Keep your attention on maintaining smooth and rhythmic breathing throughout the entire sequence of movements.

8. Rest.

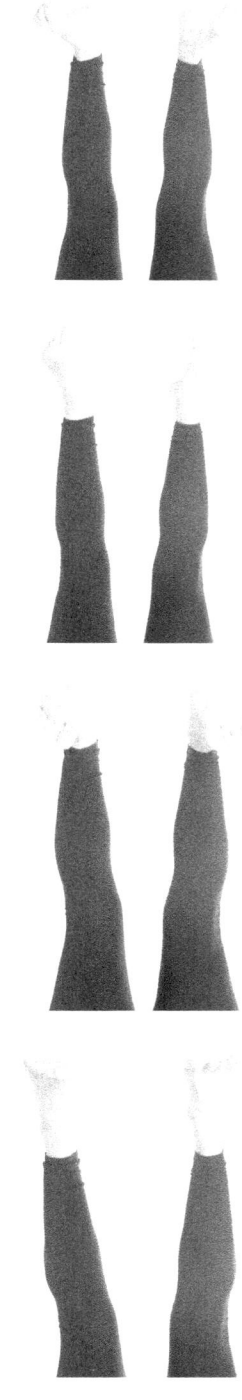

SAVASANA

I have shared about the importance and the meaning of this posture in Chapter 10. I will have to reiterate—DO NOT SKIP THIS POSTURE! The benefits are far greater than any drawbacks that I have ever experienced in either myself or my clients and students.

1. Come into resting position, lying on your spine, or rest in a comfortable position that you can tolerate.
2. Place a small pillow or rolled up towel behind your knees for support (optional when on your back).
3. Let go of any structured breathing. Allow your body to rest and to return to your natural breathing rhythm.
4. Allow your arms and legs to rest completely along your sides.
5. Palms face up.
6. Eyes are closed, as you are comfortable.
7. A light blanket or sheet may be used to cover your body to keep it warm.
8. Rest for at least five minutes at the end of a therapeutic yoga practice.

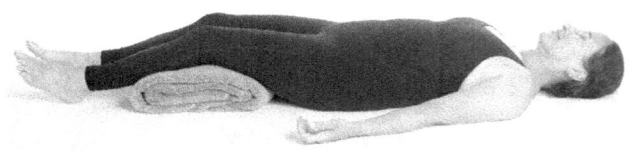

SAVASANA: PROGRESSIVE HEALING RELAXATION

Move into a comfortable and supported position on the mat. Use any support under your body that might make you more comfortable. Stretch your arms and legs out. Allow your palms to face skyward. Close your eyes. With your mouth closed, breathe softly through your nose, if possible.

Rest.

Allow your body to relax. We will focus our attention on healing and renewing each cell in your body as you rest. Breathe in, breathe out.

Let your body drop into the mat. Allow yourself to relax as you inhale and exhale.

Close your eyes, and begin to draw your attention to the sensation of the breath moving through your entire body. Feel your belly rise and fall as you breathe and feel the gentle movement of your ribs as you breathe in and out.

Visualize the process of healing that is happening within your body. Life-sustaining oxygen moving easily into the cells of each part of your body as it relaxes. Breathe in, breathe out.

Continue rhythmic and gentle breathing, and bring your attention to the muscles on your face. With each exhalation feel the muscles release and relax. Encourage your body's natural ability to heal itself while you rest. Breathe in, breathe out.

Bring your attention to the muscles around your neck and shoulders. With each exhalation, feel the muscles release and relax. Encourage your body's natural ability to heal itself while you rest. Breathe in, breathe out.

Bring your attention to the muscles in your upper arms, forearms, and hands. With each exhalation feel the muscles release and relax. Encourage your body's natural ability to heal itself while you rest. Breathe in, breathe out.

Bring your attention to the muscles in your torso, the abdominal and rib muscles, and the muscles along your spine, hips, and pelvis. With each exhalation, feel the muscles release and relax. Encourage your body's natural ability to heal itself while you rest. Breathe in, breathe out.

Bring your attention to the muscles in your thighs, front and back, the lower legs, and feet. With each exhalation, feel the muscles release and relax. Breathe in, breathe out. Encourage your body's natural ability to heal itself while you rest for the next few minutes. Feel the prana, the life force, move through your entire body as you rest, relax, and renew yourself in this savasana. Breathe in, breathe out.

(Rest for 10 minutes.)

(Come out of the relaxation.)

Bring your awareness back to this space where you are resting.

Bring gentle movement awareness to your fingers and toes, as you lie on the mat bringing awareness back to your body that has been resting in this space. Connect with your body.

Inhale, and stretch your arms overhead. Exhale, and slowly bend your knees.

Gradually roll onto your side. Hold here in this position. Breathe in, breathe out.

Slowly come up into the seated posture. You can sit tall up on your blanket or on the floor. Come into the simple sitting position where one leg is gently crossed in front of the other, or any comfortable sitting position that honors you. Breathe and be at peace.

WALKING OUTDOORS

Take a moment to take a walk outdoors as often as possible. If you are not sure how to start, begin with a two-minute walk in one direction. Stop. Turn around, and return to where you started. This is a beginning.

Make sure that you are wearing comfortable and supportive shoes, and keep awareness that the surface that you are walking on is clear of any obstacles. Practice keeping attention on your ability to maintain smooth and rhythmic breathing through your nose while you walk. Use this as a mindful activity.

If you are walking outdoors, I recommend not using any listening devices or wearing earbuds or headphones that could make it difficult for you to maintain safety for your surroundings. Instead, walk mindfully, and take time to listen to the sounds of your surroundings.

Make your walking time an opportunity for a mindful walking meditation.

Make a commitment to walk regularly. Do not be in a hurry to increase the time or distance. Keep your attention on your ability to maintain smooth and rhythmic breathing while you are walking to know that you are walking at the correct speed and intensity. Take rest stops as necessary. When the amount of time begins to feel easy, increase it by a few minutes. Make increases every few weeks, as tolerated, and gradually increase the time of your walk until you feel comfortable with walking for 30 minutes.

Remember to complete your walking for exercise with a few gentle therapeutic yoga stretches. Set a realistic goal for the time or distance (including cool-down stretch) that you know fits into your daily routine. We understand that walking is an excellent form of exercise that can provide significant health benefits, but just like therapeutic yoga, it only works if you do it. Enjoy!

REFERENCES

INTRODUCTION

Hughes, D. C., **Darby, N.**, Gonzalez, K., Boggess, T., Morris, R. M., & Ramirez, A. G. (2015). Effect of a six-month yoga exercise intervention on fitness outcomes for breast cancer survivors. *Physiotherapy Theory and Practice*, *31*(7), 451–460. https://doi.org/10.3109/09593985.2015.1037409

Kaushik, D., Shah, P. K., Mukherjee, N., Ji, N., Dursun, F., Kumar, A. P., Thompson, I. M., Jr, Mansour, A. M., Jha, R., Yang, X., Wang, H., **Darby, N.**, Ricardo Rivero, J., Svatek, R. S., & Liss, M. A. (2022). Effects of yoga in men with prostate cancer on quality of life and immune response: a pilot randomized controlled trial. *Prostate Cancer and Prostatic Diseases*, *25*(3), 531–538. https://doi.org/10.1038/s41391-021-00470-w

Patel, D. I., Almeida, G. J., **Darby, N. T.**, Serra, M. C., Calderon, T., Lapetoda, A., Gutierrez, B., Ramirez, A. G., & Hughes, D. C. (2022). Therapeutic yoga reduces pro-tumorigenic cytokines in cancer survivors. *Supportive Care in Cancer*, *31*(1), 33. https://doi.org/10.1007/s00520-022-07536-y

CHAPTER ONE

Bryant, E. F. (2009). *The Yoga Sūtras of Patañjali*. North Point Press.

Carrera, J. (2020). *Inside the Yoga Sutras: A Comprehensive Sourcebook for the Study & Practice of Patanjali's Yoga Sutras*. Integral Yoga Publications.

Roach, G. M., & McNally, L. C. (2009). *The Essential Yoga Sutra: Ancient Wisdom for Your Yoga*. Three Leaves Press, Doubleday.

Woodyard, C. (2011). Exploring the therapeutic effects of yoga and its ability to increase quality of life. *International Journal of Yoga*, *4*(2), 49–54. https://doi.org/10.4103/0973-6131.85485

CHAPTER TWO

Centers for Disease Control and Prevention. (2021, August 6). *Facts About Falls*. https://www.cdc.gov/falls/facts.html

Milkman, K. (2021, November 29). *How to build a habit in 5 steps, according to science*. CNN. https://www.cnn.com/2021/11/29/health/5-steps-habit-builder-wellness/index.html

CHAPTER THREE

Birch, B. B. (2000). *Beyond Power Yoga*. Fireside.

Dinsmore-Tuli, U. (2014). *Yoni Shakti: A Woman's Guide to Power and Freedom Through Yoga and Tantra*. Yoga Words.

Farhi, D. (1996). *The Breathing Book: Good Health and Vitality Through Essential Breath Work*. Holt Paperbacks.

Garner, G. (2016). *Medical Therapeutic Yoga: Biopsychosocial Rehabilitation and Wellness Care*. Handspring Publishing Limited.

Porges, S. W. (2011). *The Polyvagal Theory: Neurophysiological Foundations of Emotions, Attachment, Communication, and Self-regulation*. W.W. Norton & Company.

CHAPTER FOUR

André, C. (2019, January 15). *Proper breathing brings better health*. Scientific American. https://www.scientificamerican.com/article/proper-breathing-brings-better-health/

Benson, H., & Proctor, W. (2010). *Relaxation Revolution*. Scribner. https://www.perlego.com/book/1406376/relaxation-revolution-the-science-and-genetics-of-mind-body-healing-pdf

Birch, B. B. (1995). *Power Yoga: The Total Strength and Flexibility Workout*. Fireside.

Cleveland Clinic. (2020, May 12). *Nervous system*. https://my.clevelandclinic.org/health/articles/21202-nervous-system

Hall, H., & Sanjaghsaz, H. (2022). *Diastasis Recti Rehabilitation*. StatPearls Publishing. https://www.ncbi.nlm.nih.gov/books/NBK573063/

Hardman, A. E., Jones, P. R. M., Norgan, N. G., & Hudson, A. (1992). Brisk walking improves endurance fitness without changing body fatness in previously sedentary women. *European Journal of Applied Physiology and Occupational Physiology, 65*(4), 354–359. https://doi.org/10.1007/bf00868140

Harvard Medical School. (n.d.). *Benefits of sleep*. https://healthysleep.med.harvard.edu/healthy/matters/benefits-of-sleep

Kelly, P., Williamson, C., Niven, A. G., Hunter, R., Mutrie, N., & Richards, J. (2018). Walking on sunshine: scoping review of the evidence for walking and mental health. *British Journal of*

Sports Medicine, 52(12), 800–806. https://doi.org/10.1136/bjsports-2017-098827

Krowiak, S. (2020, March 11). *The vagus nerve: Your superhighway to health.* Yoga International. https://yogainternational.com/article/view/the-vagus-nerve-your-superhighway-to-health/

Levine, P. A. (2010). *In an Unspoken Voice.* North Atlantic Books.

Lima, L. V., Abner, T. S. S., & Sluka, K. A. (2017). Does exercise increase or decrease pain? Central mechanisms underlying these two phenomena. *Journal of Physiology, 595*(13), 4141–4150. https://doi.org/10.1113/jp273355

McCorry, L. K. (2007). Physiology of the autonomic nervous system. *American Journal of Pharmaceutical Education, 71*(4), 78. https://doi.org/10.5688/aj710478

McGinley, K. (2015, October 22). *Why Savasana Is the hardest yoga pose.* Chopra. https://chopra.com/articles/why-savasana-is-the-hardest-yoga-pose

McGreevey, S. (2015, October 13). *Relaxation response proves positive.* Harvard Gazette. https://news.harvard.edu/gazette/story/2015/10/relaxation-response-proves-positive/

Merriam-Webster. (n.d.). Endurance. In *Merriam-Webster.com dictionary.* Retrieved May 11, 2023, from https://www.merriam-webster.com/dictionary/endurance

Michaud, M. (2016, August 8). *Study reveals brain's finely tuned system of energy supply.* University of Rochester Medical Center. https://www.urmc.rochester.edu/news/story/study-reveals-brains-finely-tuned-system-of-energy-supply

Nutrition Source. (2023, April 19). *Walking for exercise.* Harvard T.H. Chan School of Public Health. https://www.hsph.harvard.edu/nutritionsource/walking/

Riggs, S. (2012, August 19). My Brain Needs Oxygen—What Can I Do? *The NACD Foundation, 25*(5), 201. https://www.nacd.org/my-brain-needs-oxygen-what-can-i-do/

Rosenberg, Stanley. (2017). *Accessing the Healing Power of the Vagus Nerve.* North Atlantic Books.

Shnayderman, I., & Katz-Leurer, M. (2012). An aerobic walking programme versus muscle strengthening programme for chronic low back pain: a randomized controlled trial. *Clinical Rehabilitation, 27*(3), 207–214. https://doi.org/10.1177/0269215512453353

Suh, J. H., Kim, H., Jung, G. P., Ko, J. Y., & Ryu, J. S. (2019). The effect of lumbar stabilization and walking exercises on chronic low back pain: A randomized controlled trial. *Medicine, 98*(26), e16173. https://doi.org/10.1097/md.0000000000016173

Tomlinson, K. (n.d.). *Why Savasana is so important.* EkhartYoga. https://www.ekhartyoga.com/articles/practice/why-savasana-is-so-important

Van Der Kolk, B. (2014). *The Body Keeps the Score.* Penguin Books.

Watts, M. E., Pocock, R., & Claudianos, C. (2018). Brain Energy and Oxygen Metabolism: Emerging Role in Normal Function and Disease. *Frontiers in Molecular Neuroscience, 11*, 216. https://doi.org/10.3389/fnmol.2018.00216

YJ Editors (2021, October 14). *Beginners' Yoga Poses: Corpse Pose.* Yoga Journal. https://www.yogajournal.com/poses/corpse-pose-2/

CHAPTER FIVE

Birch, B. B. (1995). *Power Yoga: The Total Strength and Flexibility Workout.* Fireside.

Nachemson, A. L. (1981). Disc pressure measurements. *Spine, 6*(1), 93–97. https://doi.org/10.1097/00007632-198101000-00020

Wilke, H., Neef, P., Caimi, M., Hoogland, T., & Claes, L. E. (1999). New *In Vivo* Measurements of Pressures in the Intervertebral Disc in Daily Life. *Spine, 24*(8), 755–762. https://doi.org/10.1097/00007632-199904150-00005

CHAPTER SIX

Blazevich, A. J., Kay, A. D., Waugh, C., Fath, F., Miller, S., & Cannavan, D. (2012). Plantarflexor stretch training increases reciprocal inhibition measured during voluntary dorsiflexion. *Journal of Neurophysiology, 107*(1), 250–256. https://doi.org/10.1152/jn.00407.2011

Crone C. (1993). Reciprocal inhibition in man. *Danish Medical Bulletin, 40*(5), 571–581.

Waxenbaum, J. A., & Lu, M. (2022). *Physiology, Muscle Energy.* StatPearls Publishing. https://www.ncbi.nlm.nih.gov/books/NBK559029/

CHAPTER SEVEN

Boden, I., Skinner, E. H., Browning, L., Reeve, J., Anderson, L., Hill, C., Robertson, I. K., Story, D., & Denehy, L. (2018). Preoperative physiotherapy for the prevention of respiratory complications after upper abdominal surgery: pragmatic, double blinded, multicentre randomised controlled trial. *BMJ, 365*, j5916. https://doi.org/10.1136/bmj.j5916

Brinjikji, W., Luetmer, P. H., Comstock, B., Bresnahan, B. W., Chen, L. E., Deyo, R. A., Halabi, S., Turner, J. A., Avins, A. L.,

James, K., Wald, J. T., Kallmes, D. F., & Jarvik, J. G. (2015). Systematic Literature Review of Imaging Features of Spinal Degeneration in Asymptomatic Populations. *American Journal of Neuroradiology*, *36*(4), 811–816. https://doi.org/10.3174/ajnr.a4173

Brumagne, S., Diers, M., Danneels, L., Moseley, G. L., & Hodges, P. W. (2019). Neuroplasticity of Sensorimotor Control in Low Back Pain. *Journal of Orthopaedic & Sports Physical Therapy*, *49*(6), 402–414. https://doi.org/10.2519/jospt.2019.8489

Chevalier, G., Sinatra, S. T., Oschman, J. L., Sokal, K., & Sokal, P. (2012). Earthing: Health Implications of Reconnecting the Human Body to the Earth's Surface Electrons. *Journal of Environmental and Public Health*, *2012*, 1–8. https://doi.org/10.1155/2012/291541

Cleveland Clinic. (n.d.). *Poor circulation*. https://my.clevelandclinic.org/health/diseases/21882-poor-circulation

Davidson, K. (2021, February 17). *Yoga Inversion: A Guide to What It Is, and How You Can Benefit. Healthline*. https://www.healthline.com/nutrition/yoga-inversion - benefits

Harvard Health. (2021, November 16). *Foods that fight inflammation*. https://www.health.harvard.edu/staying-healthy/foods-that-fight-inflammation

Health Essentials Newsletter. (2021, June 15). *Eat these foods to reduce stress and anxiety*. Cleveland Clinic. https://health.clevelandclinic.org/eat-these-foods-to-reduce-stress-and-anxiety/

Katsura, M., Kuriyama, A., Takeshima, T., Fukuhara, S., & Furukawa, T. A. (2015). Preoperative inspiratory muscle training for postoperative pulmonary complications in adults undergoing cardiac and major abdominal surgery. *Cochrane Database of Systematic Reviews*, *10*. https://doi.org/10.1002/14651858.cd010356.pub2

Kiecolt-Glaser, J. K. (2010). Stress, Food, and Inflammation: Psychoneuroimmunology and Nutrition at the Cutting Edge. *Psychosomatic Medicine*, *72*(4), 365–369. https://doi.org/10.1097/psy.0b013e3181dbf489

Li, T. P., Jain, A., & Cao, X. (2021). Sources of lumbar back pain during aging and potential therapeutic targets. *Vitamins and Hormones*, *115*, 571–583. https://doi.org/10.1016/bs.vh.2020.12.022

Mansour, A. R., Farmer, M. A., Baliki, M. N., & Apkarian, A. V. (2014). Chronic pain: the role of learning and brain plasticity. *Restorative Neurology and Neuroscience*, *32*(1), 129–139. https://doi.org/10.3233/RNN-139003

Mayo Clinic. (n.d.). *Bone spurs*. https://www.mayoclinic.org/diseases-conditions/bone-spurs/diagnosis-treatment/drc-20370216

Mayo Clinic. (2022, August 11). *Peripheral neuropathy.* https://www.mayoclinic.org/diseases-conditions/peripheral-neuropathy/symptoms-causes/syc-20352061

Nutrition Source. (2021, October 22). *Diet review: Anti-inflammatory diet.* Harvard T.H. Chan School of Public Health. https://www.hsph.harvard.edu/nutritionsource/healthy-weight/diet-reviews/anti-inflammatory-diet/

Oschman, J., Chevalier, G., & Brown, R. (2015). The effects of grounding (earthing) on inflammation, the immune response, wound healing, and prevention and treatment of chronic inflammatory and autoimmune diseases. *Journal of Inflammation Research, 8,* 83–96. https://doi.org/10.2147/jir.s69656

Prissel, R. (2021, October 14). *Want to ease chronic inflammation? Start with your grocery list.* Mayo Clinic Health System. https://www.mayoclinichealthsystem.org/hometown-health/speaking-of-health/want-to-ease-chronic-inflammation

Sator-Katzenschlager, S. (2014). Pain and neuroplasticity. *Revista Médica Clínica Las Condes, 25*(4), 699–706. https://doi.org/10.1016/s0716-8640(14)70091-4

Shelerud, R. A. (2022, May 5). *Bulging disk vs. herniated disk: What's the difference?* Mayo Clinic. https://www.mayoclinic.org/diseases-conditions/herniated-disk/expert-answers/bulging-disk/faq-20058428

Taylor, M. J. (2018). *Yoga Therapy as a Creative Response to Pain.* Singing Dragon.

CHAPTER TEN

Apter, M. J. (Ed.). (2001). *Motivational styles in everyday life: A guide to reversal theory.* American Psychological Association. https://doi.org/10.1037/10427-000

Apter, M. J. (2015). Reversal theory and the structure of the emotional experience. *Stress and Emotion: Anger, Anxiety, and Curiosity,* (14), 17-30.

Apter, M. J. (1982). *The experience of motivation: A theory of psychological reversals.* Academic Press.

Brito, L. B., Ricardo, D. R., Araújo, D. S., Ramos, P. S., Myers, J., & Araújo, C. G. (2014). Ability to sit and rise from the floor as a predictor of all-cause mortality. *European journal of preventive cardiology, 21*(7), 892–898. https://doi.org/10.1177/2047487312471759

Cuevas, B. T., Hughes, D. C., Parma, D. L., Treviño-Whitaker, R. A., Ghosh, S., Li, R., & Ramirez, A. G. (2014). Motivation, exercise, and stress in breast cancer survivors. *Support Care Cancer, 22*(4), 911–917. https://doi.org/10.1007/s00520-013-2038-6

REFERENCES

Darby, N. T., Rowan, S., Calderon, T., Gonzalez, S., Almeida, G., Zhang, T., Hughes, D. H. (2021, November) *Livestream therapeutic yoga practice and cardiorespiratory function outcomes during a pandemic with adult cancer survivors* [Livestream presentation]. The Symposium on Yoga Research.

Desselles, M., Hughes, D. C., Perkins, H. Y., et al. (2013) *Motivational Profile of Female Cancer Survivors in Behavioral Clinical Research Trials* [Presentation]. 16th International Reversal Theory Conference, Reims, France.

Desselles, M. L., Murphy, S. L., Theys, E. R. (2014). The Development of the Reversal Theory State Measure. *Journal of Motivation, Emotion, and Personality*, 2(1), 10-21.

Gorina, Y., Hoyert, D., Lentzner, H., Goulding, M. (2006). Trends in causes of death among older persons in the United States. *Aging Trends*, No 6. Hyattsville, Maryland: National Center for Health Statistics. 2006. https://www.cdc.gov/nchs/data/ahcd/agingtrends/06olderpersons.pdf

Hughes, D. C., Basen-Engquist, K. M. (2006, July). *Reversal Theory and Adherence to an Exercise Program after Endometrial Cancer* [Presentation]. Instrumentation in Reversal Theory, Shreveport, LA.

Hughes, D. C., Baum, G. P., Perkins, H. Y., Basen-Engquist, K. M. (2009, July). *Metamotivational States and Exercise Behaviors in Previously Sedentary Endometrial Cancer Survivors.* [Presentation]. 14th International Reversal Theory Conference, New Orleans, LA.

Hughes, D. C., **Darby, N.**, Gonzalez, K., Boggess, T., Morris, R. M., & Ramirez, A. G. (2015). Effect of a six-month yoga exercise intervention on fitness outcomes for breast cancer survivors. *Physiotherapy Theory and Practice*, 31(7), 451–460. https://doi.org/10.3109/09593985.2015.1037409

Hughes, D. C., Ortiz, A., Garcini, L., Serra, M., Kilpela, L., Patel, D., Parma, D. L., Munoz, E., Lapetoda, A., Ramirez, A. G., Marin, J., **Darby, N.T.**, & Cuevas, B. T. (2019) Feasibility of a Pilot Study using Reversal Theory States to Test Holistic Interventions to Maximize Cancer Survivors' Quality of Life. *Journal of Motivation, Emotion and Personality*, 8(1), 6-20. https://doi.org/10.12689/jmep.2019.802

Kakara, R., Bergen, G., & Burns, E. (2023). Understanding the Association of Older Adult Fall Risk Factors by Age and Sex Through Factor Analysis. *Journal of Applied Gerontology*, 42(7), 1662–1671. Advance online publication. https://doi.org/10.1177/07334648231154881

Kaushik, D., Shah, P. K., Mukherjee, N., Ji, N., Dursun, F., Kumar, A. P., Thompson, I. M., Jr, Mansour, A. M., Jha, R., Yang, X., Wang, H., **Darby, N.**, Ricardo Rivero, J., Svatek, R. S., & Liss, M.

A. (2022). Effects of yoga in men with prostate cancer on quality of life and immune response: a pilot randomized controlled trial. *Prostate Cancer and Prostatic Diseases*, *25*(3), 531–538. https://doi.org/10.1038/s41391-021-00470-w

Levine, P. A. (2010). *In an Unspoken Voice*. North Atlantic Books.

Moreland, B. L., Legha, J. K., Thomas, K. E., & Burns, E. R. (2023). Hip Fracture-Related Emergency Department Visits, Hospitalizations and Deaths by Mechanism of Injury among Adults Aged 65 and Older, United States 2019. *Journal of aging and health*, *35*(5-6), 345–355. https://doi.org/10.1177/08982643221132450

Patel, D. I., Almeida, G. J., **Darby, N. T.**, Serra, M. C., Calderon, T., Lapetoda, A., Gutierrez, B., Ramirez, A. G., & Hughes, D. C. (2022). Therapeutic yoga reduces pro-tumorigenic cytokines in cancer survivors. *Supportive Care in Cancer*, *31*(1), 33. https://doi.org/10.1007/s00520-022-07536-y

Porges, S. W. (2011). *The Polyvagal Theory: Neurophysiological Foundations of Emotions, Attachment, Communication, and Self-regulation*. W.W. Norton & Company.

Porges, S. W. (2017). *The Pocket Guide to The Polyvagal Theory*. W.W. Norton & Company.

Porges, S. W. & Dana, D. (2018). *Clinical Applications of the Polyvagal Theory*. W.W. Norton & Company.

Rosenberg, Stanley. (2017). *Accessing the Healing Power of the Vagus Nerve*. North Atlantic Books.

Stevens, J. A., & Rudd, R. A. (2014). Circumstances and contributing causes of fall deaths among persons aged 65 and older: United States, 2010. *Journal of the American Geriatrics Society*, *62*(3), 470–475. https://doi.org/10.1111/jgs.12702

Sullivan, M., Erb, M., Schmalzl, L., Moonaz, S., Noggle, T., & Porges, S.W. (2018) Yoga Therapy and Polyvagal Theory: The Convergence of Traditional Wisdom and Contemporary Neuroscience for Self-Regulation and Resilience. *Frontiers in Human Neuroscience*, 12. DOI=10.3389/fnhum.2018.00067

Van Der Kolk, B. (2014). *The Body Keeps the Score*. Penguin Books.

ACKNOWLEDGMENTS

I would like to acknowledge and thank the persons who have influenced me and/or made the possibility of my writing this book a reality.

To my family who has supported me in every adventure over the decades. My husband, David, whose patience, and support has allowed me to follow my passions personally and professionally while keeping me grounded. Our children, Jake and Michelina, who inspire me every day with the intellect, insight, kindness, and compassion that they embody.

To my parents, Pedro (1928–2014) and Balbina (Bobbie), eternal optimists whose belief in the power of family and the importance of education and using your resources wisely guide me and my siblings to this day. They showed by their living example that wisdom comes from the experience that you gain by trying even if the odds of failure are high, and that caring and supporting others in need is just what we do. Their example is the inspiration for the name of the learning platform that supports my educational outreach and research, the Open Hand Institute.

To my amazing sisters, Norma, Nora, and Noelia, who inspire me with their creativity, loving hearts, kindness, and generosity, and allow me to be myself. My brothers, Pete, Roy, and Rick, who support and continue to tolerate their little sister to this day. I have learned so much from observing each of you over our lifetimes, and I love you dearly.

To my yoga lifestyle teacher, Beryl, who introduced me to and continues to inspire me along the Eight-Limbed Path of the yoga lifestyle. I have spent 20 years studying with, learning from, and observing Beryl. She introduced me to mindfulness and further strengthened my awareness of the breath in her approach to meditation. My life and work are positively impacted by her influence and for this I am forever grateful.

To the late Esther Vexler (1918-2016) who presented herself to me exactly when I needed her, shared that she also learned yoga from reading books, and encouraged me to begin teaching yoga to groups. We are kindred spirits. I keep her in my heart and am grateful for the amazing contributions that she and her family have made in the yoga community and to many other groups in San Antonio.

To the creators of the Yogic philosophy and practices whose origin lies within the Indian culture and spans over thousands of years. I am grateful to have the opportunity to learn from the teachers who have passed this ancient methodology down in practices, writings, and live instruction.

To Dr. Amelie Ramirez, a.k.a. "Super Woman," who invited me to join her team of cancer researchers in 2009, so that we could begin the first of many therapeutic yoga and cancer research programs that continue to this day. The work that you do to elevate the local and global Hispanic communities towards improved health inspires me every day.

To Dr. Daniel Hughes and the HEAL team of professionals who provided their services towards the goal of continuing our therapeutic yoga research and the survivors who participated in our research studies.

To the team of HEAL Therapeutic Yoga Research teachers, current and past. Your work changes the lives of many for the better.

To the many strong women who have acted as supervisors, mentors, and friends to me, showing me that a woman's worth is multi-faceted and ever-evolving. You know who you are, and I love you.

To the community of physicians, physical therapists, massage therapists, acupuncturists, chiropractors, and rehabilitation, fitness, and yoga specialists who have supported my practices in their continuing client referrals.

To the Open Hand Institute cohorts of 200- and 300-hour Therapeutic Yoga Teacher trainees that are now certified and moving about their world using portions of the Therapeutic Astanga Method© in their daily lives, movement, exercise, and yoga living skills. Your interest, support, and encouragement made writing this book seem possible. Yes, the TAM© manual is next! ☺

To Simone, Regina, Sandy, Teresa, Sarah, Vicky, and Ernest who were part of the original therapeutic yoga teaching team at my first studio. To the community of individuals who have been a fitness or therapeutic yoga client, yoga student, and follower at Nydia's Yoga Therapy Studio and the Open Hand Institute, and to my physical therapy patients who kept coming back for more.

To Sherry and Shuen Pan who presented the opportunity of opening the commercial location of my first yoga studio and to Travis, Peggy, and Cheri Basham who's support of my crazy idea, helped make it a reality. I am honored and blessed by your friendship and support.

To my editor, Nancy, who's support and insight made all the difference to me as a first-time author, to Irene whose graphic work and artistic direction in this and many other projects is a lifesaver, and to Lisa who's photography skills helped me to create a visual experience for my readers.

To the many clients that presented with spine pain and instability that had enough faith in themselves and trust in me to help them move back into functional living with less pain using therapeutic yoga. Each of you is the inspiration for this writing, and I am grateful for you.

To the future readers of this book, who might improve their functional mobility by stepping on the path of the Therapeutic Astanga Method©.

And lastly, to the individuals living with spine pain who have yet to discover that there is hope for them still as they move towards better function and less pain with therapeutic yoga.

ABOUT THE AUTHOR

Nydia Tijerina Darby is a Doctor of Physical Therapy, Therapeutic Yoga Research Specialist, Certified Yoga Therapist, published author of therapeutic yoga research, and owner and creative director of the Open Hand Institute and Nydia's Yoga Therapy Studio in San Antonio, Texas.

She has dedicated her life toward practicing what she preaches and supports her clients on their journeys toward mind, body, and spirit wholeness in the integrative physical therapy and therapeutic yoga practices that she shares.

Nydia is an experienced yoga educator and international presenter on Therapeutic Yoga Lifestyle practices. She has melded 40 years of her experiences in physical therapy, fitness, and yoga to develop the unique method of Therapeutic Yoga that is the Therapeutic Astanga Method©. This specialized therapeutic yoga approach has been featured within the interventions that she creates for therapeutic yoga and cancer research in collaboration with University of Texas Health San Antonio.

Nydia is a public speaker, presenting workshops, community education, and therapeutic yoga instruction, and she offers continuing education for rehabilitation and yoga professionals to introduce her method of therapeutic yoga lifestyle practices. She acts as a liaison between the yoga and medical communities in San Antonio and surrounding communities in Texas.

Nydia continues to offer her work to the community of individuals who might benefit from her services by providing private therapeutic yoga assessments and instruction, private physical therapy and leads small group therapeutic yoga classes on-site and via livestream at her home studio in San Antonio, Texas.

Nydia's mantras that continue to guide and influence her practices:

"I am in training for my next decade," "The ONLY thing that you have to do is BREATHE," and "Set your intention to create your reality."

You can get more information and access digital and downloadable content at TherapeuticYogaWorks.com.

THANK YOU FOR READING MY BOOK. WILL YOU DO ME A FAVOR?

I would love to hear what you have to say about what you have learned about therapeutic yoga and spine care by reading my book and would appreciate your feedback in the form of a REVIEW on Amazon.

Your input will help me to continue to grow as a writer and can help make my future books better. I check my reviews and would love to get your feedback. I want to know that this book is reaching out and helping people move away from back pain and towards a more enjoyable quality of life.

Please take two minutes now to leave a helpful review on Amazon letting me know what you thought of the book.

To leave me a review:

- You can visit TherapeuticYogaWorks.com/review, and it will take you directly to the Amazon site to leave a review.
- You can go to Amazon.com on your web browser, search for 'Therapeutic Yoga Works,' click on the link for this book, scroll down, and click on 'write a customer review.'

Thanks again for your feedback.

Be well.

Nydia